NEW YORK Chocolate Lover's GUIDE

NEW YORK
Chocolate
Lover's
GUIDE

The Best Candy, Cakes
and Chocolate Treats in Town

WILLIAM GILLEN and PATRICIA MacKENZIE
Illustrations by Sally Mara Sturman

CITY & COMPANY NEW YORK

City & Company

22 West 23rd Street

New York, NY 10010

Printed in the United States of America

Design by Leah Lococo

Library of Congress Cataloging-in-Publication Data is available upon request.

ISBN 1-885492-36-7

First Edition

NOTE TO READERS: Neither City & Company nor the authors has any
interest, financial or personal, in the locations listed in this book. No fees were
paid or services rendered in exchange for inclusion in these pages.

   While every effort was made to ensure that information regarding addresses,
phone numbers, hours, and prices was accurate and up-to-date at the time
of publication, it is always best to call ahead.

Contents

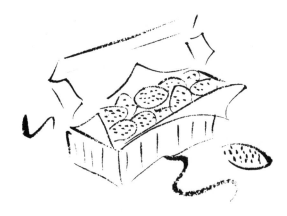

Introduction

NEW YORK IS A CHOCOLATE LOVER'S TOWN. Whatever the category—candy, cake, cookies, drinks, ice cream—if chocolate is an ingredient, then New Yorkers will passionately voice an opinion, which we discovered when we started working on this book.

Our strategy was simple: tell everyone we know that we're writing a book about chocolate in hopes of hearing about an undiscovered chocolate treasure. The reactions were enthusiastic, followed quickly by a touch of envy. When we casually mentioned the project to a hairdresser, he spontaneously shouted out the name of his favorite truffle maker. We received countless phone calls from tasting volunteers. We heard from chocolate lovers who could devour a tray of brownies in the blink of an eye. Yes, chocoholics are everywhere.

Our search for chocolate took us all over New York, from a hot chocolate street vendor's stand in the dead of winter to temporary ice cream kiosks in the heat of summer. To learn more about our favorite subject, we even visited a New Jersey manufacturing plant to see how basic chocolate is made directly from harvested cacao beans.

We sampled hundreds of chocolate candies, from the most luxurious delicacies to old-fashioned chunkies, our sources ranging from elegant Madison Avenue shops to humble stores on the Lower East Side. We tasted more chocolate cakes and cookies than we ever thought possible, starting with subtle and light creations, such as chocolate mousse desserts, and continuing on to the densest, most intense flourless cakes.

In this town, with its competitive drive and entrepreneurial spirit, new chocolate goodies are constantly popping up. We met a famous New York chef who, along with an upstate dairy man, created a chocolate butter. Not long after, we discovered a cheerful baker who makes a wonderful chocolate bread. We met scores of people whose lives revolve around chocolate. The stories they told are at the heart of the New York chocolate world.

Eat chocolate, drink chocolate, shop for chocolate, even study chocolate. We found culinary schools offering classes for those ambitious enough to learn the art of truffle making or how to bake a sophisticated cake from scratch. We were amazed at the wide selection and types of courses available in our chocolate New York.

We came to realize that the attraction to chocolate starts at an early age and only intensifies as the years go by. When we are youngsters, a chocolate candy bar is considered a treat. As we grow up, we begin to take notice of more appealing confections. How many of us remember the taste of our very first truffle? Now the quest for new and enticing chocolate creations is never ending.

Why is chocolate so addictive? Some researchers tell us it is an aphrodisiac, while others claim it stimulates the brain. Who really knows? A single piece of chocolate can curb the appetite, pacify a craving, or give us a jolt of energy. Chocolate is everything: exotic, fragrant, luscious, and on occasion even a bit sexy.

So what chocolate treat is best? Ultimately, it comes down to what pleases you most. Some days it might be nothing less than a rich bittersweet chocolate ganache made with wild raspberries, where the flavors linger like an elegant wine. At other times, a chunky chocolate-covered caramel-and-nut cluster may be immensely satisfying. Or how about the old reliable—a big, thick, still-warm-from-the-oven chocolate chip cookie along with a cold glass of milk?

The best of what we tasted can be found in this book. While we have tried to be comprehensive, at the same time we have included only those businesses that we believe are worthy of your patronage. Some famous places that, regrettably, disappointed us didn't make it into these pages.

Now, if we could only dip the Big Apple in chocolate, all those chocoholics we befriended would truly be satisfied.

How to Use This Book

THE INFORMATION PRESENTED HERE was up-to-date as this book went to press. We believe, however, that a quick telephone call is a small price to pay to ensure that a store is open or that a specific item is available on a particular day.

Store hours do fluctuate. At holiday times, when chocolate is especially in demand, some shops extend their hours; during the summer months some reduce their hours.

We've given a general idea of prices. For chocolate candy, the categories indicate price per pound as follows: Inexpensive means under $10; Moderate, $10 to $25; Expensive, $26 to $45; and Very Expensive, over $45. In other sections of the book, the categories denote a shop's prices only as they compare with those found in other businesses offering the same kind of products.

Most establishments accept major credit cards. We have indicated only those that do not.

We have also noted mail order and delivery services. We recommend that you ask specifically how purchases are sent. Some places will ship mail order only via overnight express services, and some not at all during the hot summer months. Delivery service means hand delivery within Manhattan, although some shops will arrange, for a premium price, same-day hand delivery to other areas of New York.

Finally, if a shop has at least a few cafe tables set up where you can relax and savor your treat, we have made note of it.

Luxury Chocolatiers

Who wouldn't be utterly enchanted to receive a magnificent box of chocolates? In New York, there are superlative places to find that special gift. Perhaps the delicious sweets were created by a master chocolate maker from Paris, or by a homegrown artisan who studied there. They may have been flown in from Switzerland or Belgium that very morning. One taste can conjure up the memory of a glorious vacation in Europe.

When money is no object and the aim is to impress, you can really go to town at these luxury chocolate shops. A gorgeous hand-painted box and a showpiece burl-wood case are just two of the stunning kinds of containers you can purchase to hold your precious selections.

One of the most startling revelations of our visits to the luxury chocolatiers is that you don't have to spend a lot of money in exchange for big-time enjoyment. These elegant shops will sell you a single chocolate. The city, in fact, is teeming with chocolate lovers who show up at their favorite place at the same time day after day for their one-piece fix.

So the next time you pass a luxury chocolate shop, we encourage you to walk right in, smile at the counterperson, and stand tall while ordering a single exotic truffle. It might even become a habit.

Burdick Chocolates

Mail Order and Delivery: (800) 229-2419
Prices: Expensive

WHY BEGIN A BOOK about chocolate in New York with a chocolatier from New Hampshire? Quite simply, because the chocolates made by Larry Burdick are among the best chocolates around. Besides, Burdick is no stranger to the city. He started his business in Red Hook, Brooklyn, in 1987 and later moved to East 93rd Street in Manhattan. Recently relocated to a small town in the southwest corner of New Hampshire, the company still makes weekly deliveries to a few select shops in New York, and, best of all, they'll personally deliver your order straight to your door.

Burdick views chocolate as part of the whole gastronomic experience—a nice ending to a special meal. He claims that the way to make quality chocolates is very simple: Just use the best ingredients and sell the product at its freshest.

Extracts and flavorings are taboo. Instead, coffees and teas are brewed, fresh fruits are cooked. Nuts come from California and Turkey, vanilla beans from Mexico, milk and cream from local dairies. The chocolate base, Valrhona from France, is widely considered the best available. Burdick chocolates are cut and shaped by hand, which, according to the chocolate maker, gives a more pleasant eating experience.

When you open a box of Burdick chocolates, the first surprise is their appearance. They are delicate, imperfectly shaped, and tiny—more than 70 pieces per pound. More astonishing is how wonderful they taste. Each piece melts in your mouth as the flavors unfold. There are usually at least a dozen varieties, none of which will disappoint.

The raspberry baton consists of a concentrated interior of chocolate with fresh raspberries that is covered in dark chocolate and sprinkled with finely chopped pistachios. A ginger palet is a mixture of cream and ginger root sandwiched between two thin wafers of dark chocolate, all covered in dark chocolate and subtly topped with milk chocolate flakes. Even those who snub white chocolate might become converts after tasting the ivory-with-pistachio cube. Here, crushed pistachios and a touch of lavender are added to the white chocolate to balance the sweetness.

Burdick chocolates have long been sold at Manhattan Fruitier (see page 32). More recently, the Japanese department store Takashimaya (see page 67) has been selling them too. But you can't go wrong by ordering directly from the source. Second-day air service is available, and for the same price, on Fridays only, they'll hand deliver them to Manhattan residents. What a way to start the weekend.

Christopher Norman Chocolates

Mail Order and Delivery Only: 677-3722
Hours: Monday through Friday 10:00 a.m. to 6:00 p.m.
Prices: Expensive

AN INVITATION BY PHONE to visit this start-up luxury chocolate operation took us down to a deserted cobblestone alley just off the Bowery. Once there, only the scent of chocolate brought us to the right steel-door entrance.

When the door opened, we received a warm welcome from artist John Down, who also happens to be chocolate maker Christopher Norman. His complete name is John Christopher Norman Down. One person with two careers.

The art studio down the alleyway was quickly transformed into a boutique chocolate factory after Bloomingdale's, Balducci's, Grace's Marketplace, and Nordstrom's decided to sell Christopher Norman's beautifully presented chocolates. If an exquisite package is what you yearn for, give him a call.

Christopher Norman makes 35 types of truffles, with new ones constantly being fashioned. He enjoys experimenting with offbeat flavors and introducing unusual seasonal specialties, such as an eggnog truffle during the Christmas season and a pumpkin truffle in the fall.

The walnut-rosemary truffle and the lavender-and-honey truffle are adventurous, but the herb flavorings are a little pronounced. Try the combination that he calls vanilla milk chocolate, and our hands-down favorite, the triangular-shaped dark chocolate with an oozing zabaglione center.

One of the things we like best at Christopher Norman is the ever-changing packaging, developed with a true artist's eye. Recent choices included Chinese wheat straw baskets and Japanese paper, both exquisite. An imaginative summer pebble beach box looked refreshing. Norman even writes witty notes on the pretty Mother's Day boxes.

de Granvelle Belgian Chocolatier

Prices: Expensive
Mail Order: (800) 923-5448;
Retail shops opening soon

DE GRANVELLE, an established
Belgian company, is a newcomer to the Big
Apple. Lucky for us. Their sweet, luxurious
chocolates, which come in very pretty shapes and handsome packaging, make a terrific gift.

Opening a box, it's almost impossible to decide what to try
first. Pralines, nuts, creams, mochas, solids, truffles, caramels,
and liqueur creams round out a mouth-watering assortment. We
thought we could stop at one—the milk chocolate with hazelnut
paste—but before we knew it we were on to the luscious buttercream in a heart of milk chocolate. And the pure soft caramel in
dark chocolate was wonderful too. In fact, we weren't disappointed with anything in our collection, and devoured the entire
box. De Granvelle also offers assorted potent dark chocolate cor-
dials filled with liqueurs such as Grand Marnier and kirsch.

Plans are in the works for a midtown de Granvelle shop.
And management claims that these are favorites of The Donald,
so expect to see de Granvelle kiosks in a few of the Trump
buildings soon.

5th Avenue Chocolatiere

510 Madison Ave. bet. 52nd and 53rd Sts.   935-5454
Hours: Monday through Saturday 9:00 a.m. to 6:30 p.m.
Prices: Expensive
Mail Order and Delivery Available

WHEN A PRESTIGIOUS CORPORATE JOB is ditched in favor of the pursuit of fine food, it makes for an interesting story. The story is even better when the end result is chocolates as good as those found at 5th Avenue Chocolatiere.

In the early 1970s, John Whaley was a research analyst at Morgan Guaranty. Fortuitously, he was assigned the cacao industry, through which he subsequently met Tom Krön, who comes from a long line of Hungarian chocolatiers. Whaley soon traded in his briefcase for chocolate molds when he and Krön opened a midtown shop under the Krön name in 1976. Eight years later, Whaley became sole proprietor and renamed the shop 5th Avenue Chocolatiere after its original location. The shop is now settled on Madison Avenue.

The chocolates are made in Long Island City, Queens, and are delivered to the store every day. When you walk in, chances are you'll be offered a sample of the very popular truffles, quite frequently by Whaley himself, a rotund, smiling man. His wife, Patricia, and their five children all help in running the business. The trademark truffles are dense, soft, large rectangles, dusted with cocoa powder. They are among the best around. Look on the counter, and you'll be tempted by a tray of fresh fruits dipped in chocolate. Made each morning, they fly out of the store.

The 5th Avenue Chocolatiere has more than 6,000 molds for making all kinds of chocolate novelties, from miniature typewriters and cellular telephones to life-sized business cards, soccer balls, and human legs. While many of the items have a kitschy look, the quality—especially of the dark bittersweet chocolate—is quite good. And if they don't have a mold for something you want, it can be ordered. (Chocolates from in-stock molds usually need about 24 hours advance notice; new molds, one to two weeks.) Personalized greetings can be added to many items.

Godiva Chocolatier

52 W. 50th St. (30 Rockefeller Plaza)   399-1875
Hours: Daily 9:00 a.m. to 7:00 p.m.

701 Fifth Ave. bet. 54th and 55th Sts.   593-2847
Hours: Monday through Saturday 10:00 a.m. to 7:00 p.m.;
Sunday 11:00 a.m. to 6:00 p.m.

225 Liberty St. (World Financial Center)   945-2174
Hours: Monday through Friday 10:00 a.m. to 7:00 p.m.;
Saturday 11:00 a.m. to 6:00 p.m.; Sunday Noon to 5:00 p.m.

245 Columbus Ave. bet. 71st and 72nd Sts.   787-5804
Hours: Monday through Saturday 10:00 a.m. to 9:00 p.m.;
Sunday Noon to 8:00 p.m.

560 Lexington Ave. bet. 50th and 51st Sts.   980-9810
Hours: Monday through Friday 9:00 a.m. to 7:00 p.m.;
Saturday 10:00 a.m. to 7:00 p.m.; Sunday 11:00 a.m. to 6:00 p.m.

33 Maiden Lane at Nassau St.   809-8990
Hours: Monday through Friday 9:00 a.m. to 6:00 p.m.

793 Madison Ave. at 67th St.   249-9444
Hours: Monday through Saturday 10:00 a.m. to 7:00 p.m.;
Sunday 11:00 a.m. to 6:00 p.m.

200 Park Ave. at 45th St. (MetLife Building)   697-9128
Hours: Monday through Friday 8:00 a.m. to 7:00 p.m.
Prices: Expensive
Mail Order and Delivery Available

MOST NEW YORK CHOCOLATE CONNOISSEURS were intro-
duced to the so-called premium variety when they first tasted a
Godiva chocolate in 1972. At the time it was a revelation in
comparison to the run-of-the-mill candy bar.

The Godiva company started making chocolate in Belgium
more than 80 years ago. In the late 1960s Godiva was acquired
by the Campbell Soup Company. Today, most Godiva choco-

lates are made in Pennsylvania, but a few of the individual items, like the Bouchées and Rochets, are still produced in Belgium. These two are their best.

The dark chocolate Bouchée is an oversized square with a trufflelike center. A milk chocolate version is in the form of a heart. Rochets are also big, but oval-shaped, and consist of a chocolate, caramel, and hazelnut coating over a ganache center. The coatings are available in milk, dark, and white chocolates (with the milk being our preference). Bouchées and Rochets are both terrific one-piece craving killers.

The assorted chocolates are attractively packaged. In addition to the classic gift box, there is extra-fancy packaging that changes with the seasons and holidays. Both the Fifth Avenue and the Rockefeller Center shops were recently renovated with Art Nouveau decor similar to that which appeared in Belgium around the turn of the century. These two stores are always jam-packed with tourists. Sales help in all Godiva shops is always very friendly and attentive.

Because the trademark golden Godiva box has gone mass-market, you can also find Godiva chocolate almost everywhere, including department stores and gourmet shops.

L.A. Boss

230 Park Ave. at 45th St. (Helmsley Building)   661-4820
Hours: Monday through Friday 7:00 a.m. to 6:00 p.m.
Prices: Moderate to Expensive
Mail Order and Delivery Available
Cafe Seating

SMACK IN THE HEART OF THE CITY, a stone's throw from Grand
Central Station, is this combination chocolate and coffee shop.

L.A. Boss is the ideal place for the commuter in need of a
quick gift for a special chocolate lover. On one side of the glass
case are the creations of Leonidas, the famous Belgian chocolatier (see page 30). Delicious and affordable, they're highly recommended. The white chocolate with the strawberry-cream-
filled center is aptly named Irresistible.

On the other side of the case, L.A. Boss features chocolates
made in Texas by the Sweet Shop. Large is a specialty in the
Lone Star State, and a Sweet Shop truffle is the size of a golf
ball. But better than these are the brags, big nut clusters made
with plenty of gooey caramel and covered with chocolate. The
milk chocolate pecan brags are made with lots of meaty fresh
nuts. The brag created with macadamias is tasty, but the flavor
of these delicate nuts is overwhelmed by the assertive combination of chocolate and caramel.

L.A. Boss has a refrigerated case with a decent assortment

of chocolate cakes from various suppliers. It's a place for a quick pick-me-up for the midtown lunch crowd or a treat for the commuter after a tough day.

Läderach Chocolatier Suisse

Available at the stores listed below or by mail order
through Albert Uster Imports, Inc. (800) 231-8154
Prices: Very Expensive

FOR MORE THAN 65 YEARS, the Läderach family has been making chocolates in the tiny town of Glarus, right in the heart of Switzerland. It's only in the past few years that their wonderful truffles and pralines have made their way to America. We noticed them behind glass counters at Macy's, Bloomingdale's, Balducci's, and Dean & DeLuca. One bite and we were hooked.

Each taste tells you that only top-quality ingredients go into each piece of Läderach. We love the champagne truffle with its combination of milk, white, and dark chocolate; the dark chocolate filled with a black tea ganache; and the hazelnut and milk chocolate praline.

Each piece is creatively designed and executed with Swiss precision. The chocolate cup filled with a creamy coffee ganache actually resembles a miniature cup of cappuccino. Other candies have distinct silk-screened designs, like the checkerboard square of white and milk chocolate with an almond and hazelnut filling. And some have multi-layered interiors, like the white chocolate heart filled with raspberry and dark chocolate.

Läderach candies come in a fairly even assortment of white, milk, and dark chocolates. Fans of super-bittersweet creations might be a bit disappointed with their pronounced sweetness, but we think they're great. Try them. Offer an assortment at the end of the meal at your next dinner party. We guarantee that the box will disappear in no time at all.

La Maison du Chocolat

25 E. 73rd St. bet. Fifth and Madison Aves.   744-7117
Hours: Monday through Friday 10:00 a.m. to 6:30 p.m.;
Saturday 10:00 a.m. to 6:00 p.m.
Prices: Very Expensive
Mail Order and Delivery Available

IT WAS A GREAT DAY FOR NEW YORK chocolate lovers when Robert Linxe, the famous French chocolatier, opened this little shop in 1990. Inside, the woodwork is a handsome contrast to the gold-dotted mirrors and the sparkling marble floor.

The luxurious chocolates are made of the finest ingredients, without preservatives or sugar, in one of Linxe's three Paris shops. Even the cream that goes into the truffles is the lightest, with the least fat content, available.

These confections are flown over once a week in elegant brown airtight boxes. Linxe is very proud of his innovative herb-flavored chocolate ganache, and he uses only fresh herbs: fennel, ginger, and mint. The mint is like having a single spearmint leaf placed on your tongue.

The master chocolate maker, who is also an opera buff, names his exotic creations after some of opera's masterpieces. Behind the glass counter you may spot Traviata (almond praline in dark chocolate), Othello (a ganache flavored with mountain honey), Bohème (milk chocolate ganache with a milk chocolate covering), and Rigoletto (caramelized butter covered in milk or dark chocolate). One is more voluptuous than the next.

Linxe typically visits New York four times a year. This very congenial man has a passion for his work. (We last saw him arranging a window display of yellow roses around his incredible chocolate Easter eggs.) He is a perfectionist in every way down to the raspberries he selects from the fall crop only, for those, he says, are the ones not burned by the sun. Linxe takes particular pride too in the ultra-thin chocolate coverings and the satiny smooth interiors of his confections.

According to Linxe, "The taste of chocolate should always linger." And of course it does. His personal favorite? It's called Bacchus, and consists of an exotic but subtle rum-flavored ganache wrapped in dark chocolate.

Recently he perfected a hot chocolate drink that was more than three years in the making before it pleased him enough to be sold in bottles at the shop.

Bravo to Robert Linxe and his magnificent chocolate.

∼ Robert Linxe's Hot Chocolate ∼

Robert Linxe, the creator of the sublime chocolates sold at La Maison du Chocolat, offered us his terrific hot chocolate recipe. You'll be amazed at the rich, sophisticated taste of this drink since it doesn't contain any cream or sugar (except for the sugar in the chocolate).

9 ounces bittersweet chocolate	1 ounce cocoa powder
3 $\frac{1}{3}$ cups milk	$\frac{1}{2}$ vanilla bean
2 cups water	

1. Chop the chocolate into small chunks with a sharp knife.
2. In a saucepan, heat the milk, water, cocoa powder, and vanilla bean over medium heat just until warm.
3. Add the chocolate and mix with a whisk until melted. Bring the mixture almost to a boil. Lower the heat and cook for an additional five to six minutes, or just until hot. Do not allow the mixture to boil. Remove the vanilla bean before serving.

Serves 6.

Leonidas

485 Madison Ave. bet. 51st and 52nd Sts.   980-2608

Hours: Monday through Friday 9:00 a.m. to 7:00 p.m.;

Saturday 10:00 a.m. to 7:00 p.m.; Sunday Noon to 6:00 p.m.

(closed Sunday in the summer)

Prices: Moderate

Mail Order and Delivery Available

LEONIDAS IS A REAL FIND for the New York chocolate lover. You'll be rewarded here with some of the most attentive service of any chocolate shop in the city, and the excellent, always fresh chocolates are a terrific buy at around $19 a pound.

The row of tiny Belgian flags in the window is the only clue that Leonidas is a chocolate company from Brussels. It was named for the founder, a Greek-born American, who settled in Brussels in 1910 and started making chocolate pralines, which in the U.S. means chocolates with a soft filled center. Now there are more than 1,500 Leonidas stores around the world, with the unobtrusive Madison Avenue boutique having opened just five years ago.

This modest, sparklingly clean shop houses one long counter reminiscent of an airline reservations desk. Smack in the center are all the chocolate pralines, made with fresh cream, and hard to resist.

The store is managed by Jacques Bergier, a tireless French-born chocolate maker's son, who is absolutely committed to pleasing his customers, many of whom are regulars. "People come in every afternoon and buy one or two pieces, akin to buying a bagel and coffee every day before work," Bergier says. The Lingot, a milk chocolate flavored with vanilla, and the Mystere, a dark chocolate with a pistachio-flavored center, are two very good choices.

Always on the go, Bergier, who has the build of a marathon runner, admits to eating a half pound of Leonidas chocolates a day! His biggest seller, the Manon Cafe, is white chocolate with coffee cream inside. Another treat is the tubular-shaped truffle that looks like a grown-up Tootsie Roll and melts in your mouth. The chocolate-covered orange peels are addictive. Bergier calls them "Belgian vitamin C." Packaging is kept tastefully simple, so the emphasis is on the quality and value of the product.

Manhattan Fruitier

105 E. 29th St. bet. Park and Lexington Aves.   686-0404
Hours: Monday through Friday 9:00 a.m. to 5:00 p.m.
Prices: Expensive to Very Expensive
Mail Order and Delivery Available

JEHV GOLD HAS SET EXACTING STANDARDS for the exquisite
fruit baskets that have been the hallmark of his business since
its inception. When he decided to sell chocolates as well, Gold
turned to Larry Burdick, considered by many to be America's
finest chocolatier (see page 16). Weekly deliveries ensure that
the stock is 100 percent fresh.

The shop itself boasts a bold, colorful, country-style decor,
complete with antique furniture, which is for sale. Scattered
about are the chocolate treasures: handsome wood boxes that
contain assorted chocolates, a new selection of tea-infused
chocolates, chocolate bars wrapped with ribbon, chocolate-
dipped ginger, and bags of dark French chocolate for making
hot chocolate. Around the holidays, there's usually a special-
order trio of chocolate treats that makes for a wonderful gift.

Gold acquires the finest dried pear wafers to send to his
friend Burdick in New Hampshire for dipping in chocolate.
They are an exclusive at Manhattan Fruitier, and a treat not to
be missed.

Neuchatel Chocolates

768 Fifth Ave. at Central Park South (Plaza Hotel)   751-7742
Hours: Monday through Friday 9:00 a.m. to 10:00 p.m.;
Saturday 9:30 a.m. to 10:00 p.m.; Sunday 9:30 a.m. to 7:00 p.m.

60 Wall St. bet. Pearl and William Sts.   480-3766
Hours: Monday through Friday 10:00 a.m. to 6:00 p.m.
Prices: Expensive
Mail Order and Delivery Available

"WE ARE OPEN EVERY DAY INCLUDING CHRISTMAS DAY."
Important information for anyone who enjoys chocolate on the
high-end price scale and is in need of a fix or a gift on a holiday
or late in the evening. We got this tip from John Gibbons, the
colorful store manager of the Neuchatel chocolate shop located
in the lobby of the Plaza Hotel.

Tourists flock to the tiny Victorian dollhouse of a shop,
which is strewn with teddy bears, hand-painted boxes, wicker
baskets topped with flowers, heart-shaped boxes with tapestry
coverings, golden insects, and plenty of ribbons and lace.

Neuchatel chocolates are made by a fifth-generation Swiss
chocolatier now living and working in Pennsylvania.
Approximately 19 different varieties of truffles are displayed
here behind the glass counter. In a place this size, their fra-
grance fills the shop. The most popular item is the dark champagne truffle dusted with powdered sugar. A special Grand

Passion truffle is featured around Valentine's Day. An assortment of basic milk chocolates is always available.

Neuchatel will ship or deliver in the U.S. and abroad for a additional charge. The Wall Street branch, which carries the same array of sweets, has more conservative hours for the business crowd.

Ortrud Münch Carstens

Available at the stores listed below and at Marion Design for Dining:
401 E. 58th St. bet. First Ave. and Sutton Place (212) 888-0894
Hours: Tuesday through Saturday 11:00 a.m. to 6:30 p.m.;
Sunday 1:00 p.m. to 5:00 p.m.; other times by appointment
Prices: Very Expensive
Delivery Available

LOOKING FOR SOMETHING SWEET for that special carpenter in your life? You needn't search further than the creations of Ortrud Münch Carstens. Her signature "rusty tools" are bittersweet chocolates shaped like small hammers, saws, and other implements and carefully covered with three dustings of cocoa powder for an authentic rusty look.

German-born Carstens was working in an architectural firm here 10 years ago when she had, as she calls it, "an illumination." Since then, she's been making chocolates using the finest ingredients and "labor-intensive, nineteenth-century techniques." Her rusty tools and truffles are also sold at Dean & DeLuca (see page 54), and she designs one-of-a-kind chocolate creations for large-scale events catered by Food in Motion (telephone 766-4400).

Carstens recently teamed up with Marion Design for Dining, a charming Sutton Place shop that is filled with new, antique, and custom items for the tabletop. The shop usually has a few selections of Carstens' standard offerings in stock, including chocolate ice-cream spoons, so you can have your dessert spoon and eat it too. Owner Marion will work with you to create a one-of-a-kind gift, such as an antique dish filled with truffles, and she takes special orders for unique items like that chocolate sculpture centerpiece you absolutely must have for your next dinner party.

Perugina Shoppe

520 Madison Ave. bet. 53rd and 54th Sts.   688-2490
Hours: Monday through Friday 10:00 a.m. to 6:00 p.m.;
Saturday 11:00 a.m. to 5:00 p.m.
Prices: Moderate to Expensive
Mail Order and Delivery Available

ALTHOUGH PERUGINA CONFECTIONS are widely available at many shops around town, you owe it to yourself to stop in at this delightful flagship store on Madison Avenue. This is Perugina's only retail store anywhere in the world. Designed in the style of a vintage confectionery shop, the spacious, bright, sophisticated place has a distinctly Italian flavor, from the ochre-colored walls to the charming salespeople who thank you with a "Grazie."

Oversized gift boxes in different themes contain assorted chocolates, many wrapped in colorful foils. Holidays bring out even more festive packaging.

The gold-wrapped whole hazelnuts and almonds covered in chocolate are good. But after sampling the gamut of Perugina chocolates, our favorite is still the ubiquitous Baci (Italian for kisses). These balls of whipped milk chocolate blended with chopped hazelnuts, topped with a whole hazelnut, and enrobed in bittersweet chocolate are wrapped in silver-and-blue foil and come with a love note inside.

Richart Design et Chocolat

7 E. 55th St. bet. Fifth and Madison Aves.

371-9369; (800) Richart

Hours: Monday through Friday 10:00 a.m. to 7:00 p.m.;

Saturday 10:00 a.m. to 6:00 p.m.; Sunday 11:00 a.m. to 5:00 p.m.

Prices: Very Expensive

Mail Order and Delivery Available

IF THE MUSEUM OF MODERN ART were to open a chocolate boutique, Richart would fit the bill. The company has been making chocolates in Lyons, France, for more than 70 years, but their designs and flavors are most definitely contemporary.

This midtown boutique, the only Richart shop in the United States, receives daily shipments directly from the source. Its modern white decor and the glossy white packaging make for an elegant backdrop to the sleek, silky chocolates, which are adorned with subtle hand-applied silk-screened designs.

The nice thing about this type of elegance is that it can be affordable. Yes, you can spend $1,200 on a tabletop burl-wood vault with drawers containing assorted chocolates; but for less than $2, you can also walk away with a single bonbon, such as the classic chocolate creation made with fillings ranging from traditional *framboise* (raspberry) to cutting-edge pineapple mousse, hazelnut laced with curry, or ganache with clove. We go wild for the ganache with cream and candied clementines.

The most popular gift item, the Petits Richart collection, is a small, square box containing 36 tiny filled chocolates that are about half the size of the regular bonbons. But we love the box of *ultra-fines* — 72 chocolate wafers that are designed for tasting. Each box holds stacks of nine different types of wafers with the name of the cacao bean, country of origin, and proportion of cacao content silk-screened on each piece. One thin wafer goes a long way in satisfying a craving.

Looking for a gift for the child who has everything? Richart even has bonbons for children, sweeter and less expensive than the adult versions.

To round out the selection, there's baking chocolate, cocoa powder, and an outstanding chocolate ice cream made by the restaurant Lutèce.

Teuscher Chocolates of Switzerland

25 E. 61st St. bet. Madison and Park Aves.   751-8482

Hours: Monday through Saturday 10:00 a.m. to 6:00 p.m.

620 Fifth Ave. at Rockefeller Center   246-4416

Hours: Monday through Saturday 10:00 a.m. to 6:00 p.m.; except

Thursday 10:00 a.m. to 7:30 p.m.

Prices: Very Expensive

Mail Order and Delivery Available

ONE COULD CLAIM that Teuscher Chocolates of Switzerland was the birthplace of the ultrafancy truffle in New York. The Madison Avenue shop opened its doors in 1976, and two years later a branch in Rockefeller Center appeared on the scene.

Teuscher carries 12 different varieties of truffles, but their famous champagne truffle outsells any one of the others by about 20 to 1. All are perfectly displayed and handled with extreme care.

According to Bernard Bloom, the owner of both shops, Teuscher truffles, which are made in Zürich, have only a 10-day shelf life. Ingredients include fresh cream and butter, and yes, real champagne is used in the filling of the house specialty— although the alcohol content is less than $\frac{1}{2}$ percent.

A box of assorted pralines is attractively packaged in a bright-red map of 1576 Zürich, and a combination of truffles and pralines comes in a box with a nostalgic picture of Lake

Zürich on the front. Both make nice gifts. Teuscher is very high quality chocolate, and the owner is proud that it's close to the most expensive in all of New York.

The store's decorations, also made in Switzerland, are a big part of the Teuscher shopping experience. Colorful silk and paper flowers, which change with the seasons, are draped everywhere, giving these two cozy little shops a festive appearance.

You can also buy porcelain-faced clowns, cute paper dolls, or animal figures that come with little boxes filled with your own chocolate selections. Some shoppers collect them to bring the fantasy home. Buying chocolate at Teuscher is like visiting Santa's workshop all year-round.

Old-fashioned Candy Shops

We love to visit the old-fashioned chocolate shops that have been around New York for decades. If the gems at luxury chocolatiers are meant for special occasions, then the goodies at these places are perfect for everyday enjoyment. These are the landmarks for the chocolate-covered marshmallows, the nonpareils, and the homemade fudge that we all used to eat as kids.

The shops have a timeworn charm and a feeling of comfort. You might notice in some that the wallpaper is peeling or the linoleum is threadbare with age. But as you breathe in the delicious aroma of melted chocolate, you realize that you wouldn't change the setting for the world.

Fathers have handed down businesses to sons and daughters; husbands and wives work side by side. You won't find one of these stores at a high-rent fancy address; rather, they are part of the fabric of their neighborhoods.

Quite often the candies are made right in the back of the shop, so you can sometimes catch a glimpse of the action. Occasionally, the shopkeeper might even invite you back for a tour. Maybe you'll see how molded chocolates are made. Some stores have hundreds, if not thousands, of molds they've been collecting over the years.

At holiday time, these shops are especially festive. Big, red, heart-shaped boxes decorate the windows for Valentine's Day, lovely baskets and jumbo chocolate eggs are displayed at Easter, and, of course, jolly chocolate Santas abound at Christmastime.

New York's old-fashioned chocolate shops are city treasures. It's up to all of us to keep them going.

Economy Candy

108 Rivington St. bet. Ludlow and Essex Sts.
254-1531; (800) 352-4544
Hours: Monday through Friday and Sunday 8:30 a.m.
to 5:30 p.m.; Saturday 10:00 a.m. to 5:00 p.m.
Prices: Inexpensive
Mail Order Available

ECONOMY CANDY is a delightful shop that dates back to 1937. Jerry Cohen, the amiable presence normally behind the cash register, co-owns the shop with his wife, Ilene.

The bright-blue awning out front beckons you into a wonderland of candy. This is the kind of shop that kids love and that brings out the child in any adult. The store is always busy, and around holidays, especially Halloween, it is jam-packed.

Candy is piled up everywhere. The best chocolates are in the glass case next to the cash register. Handmade by Cohen's cousin in Brooklyn, these big, fresh, chunky candies sell for less than $10 per pound. Try delicious milk chocolate–covered walnut and caramel clusters, buttercrunch, and dark chocolate–covered marshmallows, which we like to take home to freeze before eating.

There's a large kosher selection, and every year during the weeks prior to Passover, fresh chocolate-covered macaroons are stacked high by the counter.

Elk Candy Co.

240 E. 86th St. bet. Second and Third Aves.   650-1177

Hours: Monday through Saturday 9:00 a.m. to 6:45 p.m.;

Sunday 10:00 a.m. to 5:45 p.m.

Prices: Moderate; No Credit Cards

Mail Order Available

ELK CANDY has been serving its classic chocolate and marzipan treats to Yorkville residents since 1935. There have been several owners over the years, but now 25-year-old Anton Lulgjuraj is at the helm. He took over from his late father, who, prior to buying the place, had worked at Elk Candy for a quarter of a century.

The candies are made right in the back, so the aroma of chocolate always seems to fill the air of this timeworn little shop. The popular truffles and nicely boxed sets of assorted chocolates are very good, and they are value-priced at just under $20 per pound.

We especially like the kringles—round swirls of milk or dark chocolate topped with colored sprinkles—and anything here with a chocolate-marzipan combination, like the chocolate-covered marzipan with a thin layer of raspberry. The dark chocolate–covered cherries are delicious, as is the chocolate-covered toffee. Stop in the next time you're in the neighborhood. A quarter pound of chocolates, about seven pieces, will set you back less than $5.

Evelyn's Chocolates

4 John St. bet. Broadway and Broad St.   267-5170

Hours: Monday through Friday 7:30 a.m. to 6:30 p.m.

Prices: Moderate

Mail Order and Delivery Available

OLD-FASHIONED DIPPED AND MOLDED CHOCOLATES are the prime attraction at this little Financial District shop. Pop in at lunchtime and see the local business people lining up for their favorite selections, while workers dip chocolates in the tiny manufacturing area in the back of the store.

David Lazar opened up the shop in the 1940s and named it for his daughter. Twenty years later, she took over the business. Today, Evelyn Robb is still proud of her candies, and she likes to point out the popular items — buttercrunch, truffles, and molded chocolates — to new visitors. If you're in the neighborhood, you won't go wrong with a visit to Evelyn's. Treat yourself to a few pieces of whatever catches your eye.

If you're in the market for some chocolates in the guise of erotica, you've definitely arrived at the right place. With a coy smile and the wink of an eye, Robb proudly shows her photo album filled with pictures of anatomically correct chocolates that can be special ordered. It just proves that chocolate comes in all shapes and sizes.

Li-Lac Chocolates

120 Christopher St. bet. Bleecker and Hudson Sts.   242-7374
Hours: Monday through Saturday 10:00 a.m. to 8:00 p.m.;
Sunday Noon to 6:00 p.m. Summer Hours: Tuesday through
Saturday Noon to 8:00 p.m.; Sunday Noon to 6:00 p.m.
Prices: Moderate
Mail Order and Delivery Available

NOT MUCH HAS CHANGED IN THE SHOP since it opened in
1923. All chocolates are still made by hand and packaged in the
back of the store. This Greenwich Village institution is known by
everyone in the neighborhood, and so what if some of the lilac-
motif wallpaper is starting to peel: It's the chocolate that counts.

The chocolate-making process starts in an ancient copper
"cooker," then the warm chocolate is spread on a big marble slab
to rest. If you peer into the back of the shop, the work can be
observed firsthand. The chocolates are cooled on a long convey-
or belt, just like the one in the old *I Love Lucy* episode in which
Lucy, who is working in a chocolate factory, quickly starts eating
up candy when she can't keep pace with the moving conveyor.

"Lucy would have stood right there at the end," explained
store manager Maroun Chalhoub, who even keeps a photo of
the famous Lucy gag on display behind the counter. Chalhoub
has been running things at Li-Lac these past ten years. He
learned the trade from an old-timer who worked for many years

at Li-Lac and claimed he was born inside a chocolate factory in Poland.

Some of our favorites here are the bittersweet orange peels made with fruit from Australia and the delicious nut fudge that is cooked in very small batches. This is wholesome fudge that your grandmother would be proud to call her own. The fresh butter-crunch, almond bark, and coconut clusters belong in the New York Chocolate Hall of Fame. They taste deliciously homemade.

Li-Lac has plenty of specialty molds on hand for making chocolate in various shapes, from bunnies and cupids to violins, cars, and even a fireman's hat. Old-fashioned metal molds that were made in Germany are still used. Each year the shop makes the animal that symbolizes the Chinese New Year.

Come visit Li-Lac and you'll feel like a kid again.

Mondel Chocolates

2913 Broadway bet. 113th and 114th Sts.   864-2111
Hours: Monday through Saturday 11:00 a.m.
to 7:00 p.m.; Sunday Noon to 6:00 p.m.
Prices: Moderate
Mail Order Available

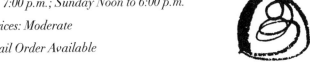

PASS BY MONDEL, and if the door is open, you'll be treated to an irresistible whiff of chocolate. Most of the candy is made in the back of this little shop, which has been in the same family since it opened in 1944. While most of the customers are students from Columbia University and residents of Morningside Heights, there are chocolate-loving New Yorkers who will travel uptown just to shop here. Around holidays, the line stretches out the door.

Christmastime brings out the Santas, and Valentine's Day, heart-shaped boxes filled with freshly made assorted chocolates. Our favorite time to visit, though, is right before Easter, when the shelves are brimming with plush bunnies and all the traditional makings for a lovely Easter basket. Don't miss the bittersweet chocolate-covered coconut eggs and the tiny milk chocolate bunnies that are filled with a terrific caramel. If you're shopping for a Passover gift, Mondel has a lovely selection of nuts and dried fruits that can be paired with their kosher chocolates.

Year-round favorites at Mondel are fudge with or without nuts, dark chocolate coconut mounds, and turtles, which are nut, caramel, and chocolate clusters.

Wolsk's Gourmet Confectioner

81 Ludlow St. bet. Broome and Delancey Sts.

475-0704; (800) 692-6887

Hours: Monday through Thursday 9:00 a.m. to 5:00 p.m.;

Friday 9:00 a.m. to 3:00 p.m.; Sunday 9:00 a.m. to 5:00 p.m.

Prices: Inexpensive

Mail Order Available

THE BIG GREEN SIGN above the store reads "Since 1939," so this Lower East Side place that calls itself a gourmet confectioner must be doing something right.

Wolsk's carries a neat selection of fresh hand-dipped treats such as chocolate-covered apricots, marshmallows, and pretzels. Pecan clusters are good and fresh, with big meaty nuts stuck together with plenty of caramel. If gooey is to your liking, Wolsk's is going to work out fine.

The store does a big mail order business, so you might find it convenient to shop by phone, as the in-store service can be a bit gruff. Keep Wolsk's in mind for Halloween. You can pick up all kinds of goodies ideal for a party or for trick or treat.

Food Emporiums

New York has a variety of food emporiums unequaled in any other city in the world. Demanding New Yorkers, who always seem to be in a hurry, flock to these shops for one-stop convenience and for the best selections of premium foods. And tourists, with cameras dangling from their necks, ooh and aah over the food displays.

On a good day, these places are bustling; around holidays, they can be perilous, with carts heading for a collision course. But where else can you find a delicious cake by a top New York baker, terrific brownies by another, fabulous truffles imported from Switzerland, lovely chocolate gelato, beautifully packaged gift boxes of candies, chunks of premium Belgian chocolate for baking, and authentic Dutch cocoa, all in one place, at one time?

Convenience has its price. All but a few of these emporiums charge top dollar for the quality and selection they proffer. And one caveat: freshness can vary considerably at the same store from day to day. When buying baked goods, always ask how long an item has been around. Since most come from outside sources, a cake may have just been delivered, or it may have been sitting in a case long after its peak. For the price you pay, you deserve the best.

Agata & Valentina

1505 First Ave. at 79th St.   452-0690
Hours: Monday through Friday 9:00 a.m. to 9:00 p.m.;
Saturday and Sunday 8:00 a.m. to 9:00 p.m.
Prices: Expensive
Mail Order and Delivery Available

AT THIS HIGH-END UPPER EAST SIDE Italian food emporium, the chocolate comes in all different shapes and sizes. Christopher Norman Chocolates (see page 18) is the chief truffle supplier for their loose chocolate section. On our last visit, we sampled a sweet chocolate truffle made with blood-orange flavoring. You can buy just one, if you wish.

The in-store baker from Italy makes a chocolate espresso explosion cake that is sold whole or by the slice. It is dense and light at the same time, with a very refined chocolate flavor and only a hint of coffee, which comes through in the aftertaste. It is the best chocolate item in the store and is nicely complemented by a good cup of strong coffee.

The jumbo chocolate-covered strawberries are available year-round. The premium dark chocolate coating is a perfect contrast to the fruit.

In the summer months, a cool and refreshing chocolate granita is available, made with syrup imported from Italy.

Balducci's

424 Sixth Ave. at 9th St.   673-2600
Hours: Daily 7:00 a.m. to 8:30 p.m.
Prices: Expensive
Mail Order and Delivery Available

THIS WORLD-FAMOUS GREENWICH VILLAGE food bazaar always has a good selection of individual chocolates and truffles. The predominant brands are Christopher Norman, made in New York, and Läderach, imported from Switzerland. The

Läderach are delicious, elegant, traditional confections; Christopher Norman offers innovative flavors, seasonal specialties, and wonderful packaging for holidays.

At Christmas and Easter, there are always a few very large, over-the-top chocolate creations, usually from Perugina, for those wanting to make a grandiose statement.

At the dessert department, you can always count on at least a dozen varieties of chocolate cakes. Notable are the selections from Black Hound, including their triple mousse cake and the single-serving chocolate basket filled with almond cake, lemon custard, whipped cream, and fresh fruit.

Dean & DeLuca

560 Broadway at Prince St.   431-1691
Hours: Monday through Saturday 8:00 a.m.
to 8:00 p.m.; Sunday 9:00 a.m. to 7:00 p.m.
Prices: Moderate to Very Expensive
Mail Order and Delivery Available
Coffee Bar (standing only)

ONE OF NEW YORK'S PREEMINENT FOOD EMPORIUMS, Dean & DeLuca probably has the most varied selection of high-quality chocolate products in town.

A glass case boasts about a dozen brands of fine confections—Caffarel Prochet from Italy, Läderach from Switzerland, and Valrhona from France, to name just a few. Noteworthy are the truffles and "rusty tools" made by New York chocolatier Ortrud Münch Carstens (see page 34)—delicious and rarely found around town, they're a wise choice at Dean & DeLuca.

The pastry area features an ever-changing selection of chocolate cakes from top metro area bakers sold both whole and in single servings. Other treats include slabs of fudge, brownies, chocolate-dipped macaroons, and double chocolate chip cookies.

Home bakers looking for block chocolate will find a good variety of Belgian Callebaut and a smaller selection of French Valrhona and Venezuelan El-Rey. The store also stocks a solid selection of Mexican, Spanish, French, Dutch, and American cocoa powders. Jars of chocolate dessert sauces, dipping sauces, and hot fudge are on a nearby shelf.

The espresso bar usually sells cups of good, rich hot chocolate. On occasion, white hot chocolate is available too. But unless you're a die-hard white chocolate fan, you'll be eminently more satisfied with the regular version.

If you're still craving chocolate when you arrive at the bakery-side checkout counter, don't fret. There are more than 50 types of premium-quality chocolate bars stacked up for that last-minute impulse purchase.

NOTE: There are several Dean & DeLuca coffee bars

throughout the city where some of the chocolate desserts and hot chocolate can be enjoyed in a cafe setting.

Fairway

2127 Broadway bet. 74th and 75th Sts.   595-1888

Hours: Daily 7:00 a.m. to Midnight

2328 12th Ave. at 132nd St.   234-3883

Hours: Monday through Thursday 8:00 a.m. to 10:00 p.m.;

Friday through Sunday 8:00 a.m. to Midnight

Prices: Inexpensive to Moderate

Delivery Available from uptown store only

SHOPPING AT THE ORIGINAL UPPER WEST SIDE market is a challenge for any New Yorker. Most of the time it is a game of bump-and-run with the baskets and carts, and right before any big holiday the place is chaotic. What saves this store from calls for the riot squad is the Fairway checkout people—quick and exacting.

Fairway carries blocks of French Cacao Barry baking chocolate—milk, bittersweet, semisweet, and white—that can be bought in broken chunks.

When you walk in, look for the fast-moving, reliable Entenmann's chocolate cakes and doughnuts in the familiar white boxes. In the bakery area at the rear, warm-from-the-oven chocolate chip cookies are sold.

Fraser-Morris

1264 Third Ave. bet. 72nd and 73rd Sts.   288-2727; (800) 423-3571
Hours: Monday through Saturday 8:30 a.m. to 6:00 p.m.
Prices: Expensive to Very Expensive
Mail Order and Delivery Available

ALL CHOCOLATES AT FRASER-MORRIS come prepackaged from both famous and not-so-famous sources and are sold at a wide range of prices. The shop is particularly festive during the Christmas holidays.

There is an impressive variety of chocolate candy made by old-time Koppers of Manhattan and packaged in round Fraser-Morris see-through plastic containers. According to owner Eric Rosenthal, the big sellers are the hand-dipped orange peels and the dried apricots. The store even carries that old New York standby, nonpareils. The colors of the sprinkles on top change with the seasons. Rosenthal was proud to mention that he even has Mother's Day nonpareils. We like the way this ensures freshness.

If you fancy imported chocolates, you can pick up boxes of Neuhaus chocolates from Belgium and Lindt from Switzerland. Best of all, in early fall, Fraser-Morris receives a limited number of truffles from Fauchon, the famous Paris gourmet shop. Fraser-Morris is the only shop in New York that carries them.

Should Fraser-Morris happen to be out of the Fauchon

truffles, pick up a box of the popular chocolate-covered marsh-mallows made by Schwartz, the owner of the now defunct Upper West Side chocolate shop of the same name.

Gourmet Garage

453 Broome St. at Mercer St.   941-5850
301 E. 64th St. bet. First and Second Aves.   535-6271
Hours: Daily 8:00 a.m. to 8:00 p.m. (both locations)
Prices: Moderate
Delivery Available

THIS WAREHOUSE-STYLE purveyor of exceptional produce and gourmet items has a limited chocolate repertoire, but does carry items worth noting. One warning though: stock changes frequently, so it's wise to call ahead.

Bakers will be pleased to find chunks of Belgian Callebaut chocolate, usually a variety that includes white, milk, semisweet, bittersweet, and unsweetened. Ice cream lovers will be in luck on the days when Ciao Bella's chocolate gelato or Bassett's chocolate ice cream is in stock. And for those with an over-whelming desire to binge on chocolate cake, two options are ready in the refrigerated cases at Gourmet Garage: the David Glass truffle cake and the Umanoff and Parsons mud cake. These could go head-to-head in a chocolate decadence competition.

Grace's Marketplace

1237 Third Ave. at 71st St.   737-0600; (800) 325-6126
Hours: Monday through Saturday 7:00 a.m. to 8:30 p.m.;
Sunday 8:00 a.m. to 7:00 p.m.
Prices: Expensive
Mail Order and Delivery Available

THE PRODUCE AND PREPARED FOOD DEPARTMENTS are the heart of this bustling Upper East Side shop. Chocolate, however, is given its due, although on a lesser scale.

Our favorite find at Grace's is the delicate tulip-shaped chocolate cups that are designed to be filled with a light dessert such as mousse or fresh berries. For the harried host or hostess, they can add a bit of flair to the dessert course. Look for them in the glass case that also houses loose luxury chocolates, mostly the very good Neuhaus brand from Belgium.

Around the holidays, the candy department stocks attractive novelty chocolate items, including giant handsome toy soldiers that come from Joseph Schmidt of San Francisco. In the confetteria, there is the expected assortment of chocolate cakes, individual chocolate desserts, and brownies, all made by New York bakers.

Zabar's

2245 Broadway at 80th St.   787-2000

Hours: Monday through Friday 8:00 a.m. to 7:30 p.m.;

Saturday 8:00 a.m. to 8:00 p.m.; Sunday 9:00 a.m. to 6:00 p.m.

Prices: Inexpensive to Moderate

Mail Order Available

NO STORE HAS MORE OF A NO-NONSENSE New York character than this Upper West Side super delicatessen. Maybe it's because everyone in town loves a bargain. You'll find one here in the stacks of discounted boxed chocolate from famous makers.

The high-end French Valrhona and the Italian Perugina brands are also sold at very favorable prices.

Zabar's carries the complete line of baking products from Ghirardelli, the San Francisco chocolate maker. They're good for making homemade chocolate chip cookies. Then there is the counter with our favorite, the Koppers candy line — especially the chocolate-covered espresso beans.

At the bread counter are luscious brownies from a place called Betsy's in the Bronx. A refrigerated section holds David Glass cakes (see page 79) — flourless, rich and dense.

In their own kitchen, Zabar's bakes a chocolate chip cheese strudel that is sold at the prepared foods counter. If that is not enough, at the checkout line you will be confronted by a big supply of chocolate bars from Lindt and Valrhona.

Department Stores

One may not think to go to a department store just to buy chocolate, but in this respect, some of New York's stores are in a league of their own.

Martine's wonderful chocolates can't be found anywhere in the city but at Bloomingdale's, where they are made fresh daily. You needn't wait for a trip to Belgium to have a Manon chocolate; you can make a quick stop at Bergdorf's, the only place that sells them in New York. While you're on Fifth Avenue, you might want to drop in at Takashimaya, where you can always find elegant

Japanese confections.

For an enormous selection of chocolates, there's no place like Macy's. There is a seemingly limitless selection that ranges from luxury European truffles and well-known brands like Godiva, to novelty items for children and foil-wrapped goodies to hang on the Christmas tree. All these are temptingly displayed in The Cellar, one of New York's most famous food halls.

Who wouldn't agree that a stop at the chocolate department can be a satisfying end to a shopping excursion? It's the perfect spot to treat yourself to something special, either as a pick-me-up or to celebrate a successful spree.

Bergdorf Goodman

754 Fifth Ave. at 58th St.   753-7300
Hours: Monday through Saturday 10:00 a.m. to 6:00 p.m.;
except Thursday 10:00 a.m. to 7:00 p.m.
Prices: Very Expensive
Mail Order and Delivery Available

UP ON THE SEVENTH FLOOR amidst antique furnishings, fine table linens, charming garden furniture, and sparkling silver sets, there are two rather modest glass cabinets filled with imported chocolates. Inside the smaller cabinet is the wonderful chocolate of La Maison du Chocolat (see page 27).

The featured chocolate is Manon, a Belgian import exclusive to Bergdorf's. Truffles include the spaceship look-alike called Sputnik, filled with rich chocolate ganache in one half, crème fraîche in the other. Many Manon chocolates contain crème fraîche and demand a short shelf life.

Modest purchases, such as a half dozen truffles, come in plastic sandwich bags. Larger selections are appropriately placed in a handsome package.

Bloomingdale's

1000 Third Ave. at 59th St.   705-2000;
First-floor candy shop   705-2953; Martine's   705-2347
Hours: Monday through Friday 10:00 a.m. to 8:30 p.m.;
Saturday 10:00 a.m. to 7:00 p.m.; Sunday 11:00 a.m. to 7:00 p.m.
Prices: Expensive
Mail Order and Delivery Available

BLOOMIE'S EPITOMIZES THE DEPARTMENT STORE chocolate shop in both style and selection. There are plenty of well-known brands to choose from in their street-level shop. Attractive packages of Godiva, Perugina, and Joseph Schmidt line the windows. Läderach truffles from Switzerland, the best of the lot, are behind the long glass counter.

When we jokingly asked a woman behind the counter

which was her favorite, she pointed to the ceiling and recommended Martine's—the chocolate boutique on the sixth floor. As we approached Martine's, truffle samples were graciously being given out in the main aisle.

We saw a toque-wearing chocolate maker supervising the blending of a fresh batch of dark chocolate. He had just finished making the round swirls of dark chocolate that are topped with dry roasted hazelnuts. They were our favorites, but two other good choices are the marzipan rolled in chocolate and the chocolate-coated cherries.

Martine's is exclusive with Bloomingdale's. It is the ideal place for the chocolate lover who wants top-quality chocolate freshly made on the day of purchase.

Lord & Taylor

424 Fifth Ave. at 38th St.   391-3344
Hours: Monday and Tuesday 10:00 a.m. to 7:00 p.m.;
Wednesday through Friday 10:00 a.m. to 8:30 p.m.;
Saturday 9:00 a.m. to 7:00 p.m.; Sunday 11:00 a.m. to 6:00 p.m.
Prices: Expensive
Mail Order and Delivery Available

THE EIGHTH-FLOOR CANDY BOUTIQUE is rather small, but if you are looking for a decent selection of loose Godiva chocolates, you will be happy here. A collection of Perugina gift boxes is also on display, if you need to pick up something in a hurry.

Keep an eye out for Mrs. Prindable's hand-dipped chocolate-covered apples. These are giant Washington State Red Delicious apples that have been dipped in caramel, rolled in a topping, and then dipped again in chocolate. One apple is enough for two. They sell out fast, so to avoid disappointment call the Lord & Taylor candy counter before you visit.

Macy's Herald Square

151 W. 34th St. at Broadway   695-4400;
Marketplace candy department   494-3519
Hours: Monday through Saturday 10:00 a.m.
to 8:30 p.m.; Sunday 11:00 a.m. to 7:00 p.m.
Prices: Moderate to Expensive
Mail Order Available

MAYBE IT IS THE PARADE ON THANKSGIVING DAY, or the fireworks display on the Fourth of July, but all native New Yorkers have a special place in their hearts for Macy's — The World's Largest Store.

Everything here is done on a grand scale, including the Marketplace in The Cellar, which offers plenty of chocolate.

The loose jumbo truffles made by San Francisco chocolatier

Joseph Schmidt are prominently displayed. Also available by the individual piece are imported brands like Läderach (Swiss), Leonidas and Neuhaus (Belgian), and Bayard—chocolate from a New Jersey company that is reasonably priced at under $10 a pound.

Macy's stocks gift boxes in a large variety of shapes and sizes. Some of the bigger displays include Perugina, Godiva, and Lindt. There are always a few sale items that are worth checking out.

Saks Fifth Avenue

611 Fifth Ave. at 49th St.   753-4000; Candy department   940-2283
Hours: Monday through Saturday 10:00 a.m. to 6:30 p.m.;
except Thursday 10:00 a.m. to 8:00 p.m.; Sunday Noon to 6:00 p.m.
Prices: Expensive to Very Expensive
Mail Order and Delivery Available

SAKS' STYLISH CHOCOLATE GALERIE, located on the eighth floor, has the most impressive selection of Neuhaus chocolates to be found anywhere in the city. These little wonders, import-ed from Belgium, are perfectly displayed on a pristine brass-trimmed marble counter. With more than 70 types of loose Neuhaus chocolates to choose from, we were tempted to sample one of each. Try the scrumptious Caprice, made of dark choco-late and filled with fresh vanilla cream and toffee. The Truffle

Cognac, completely covered with almonds, is enticing too. A big plus here is the serious attention paid to freshness. Pre-packaged chocolates from Godiva, Perugina, Joseph Schmidt, and Neuhaus are also available.

Take note of the single white glove used by the counterperson to handle your Neuhaus selections. It adds a touch of drama to your purchase. The affable clerk pointed out that many Saks shoppers purchase just a single piece, to enjoy on their escalator ride down to the ground floor.

Takashimaya New York

693 Fifth Ave. bet. 54th and 55th Sts.   350-0100; (800) 753-2038
Hours: Monday through Saturday 10:00 a.m. to 6:00 p.m.;
except Thursday 10:00 a.m. to 8:00 p.m.
Prices: Very Expensive
Mail Order and Delivery Available

As soon as the doorman ushers you into this elegant Japanese department store, you know that you are in for a high-end experience. The store clearly caters to the well-heeled, but you won't feel out of place if you've come only to buy a few pieces of chocolate or a small box of confections.

Head down to the lower level, where the international tea and chocolate shop resides alongside the Japanese tearoom.

While you might expect pretentious service, just the opposite holds true. The knowledgeable salespeople are genuinely pleasant and helpful.

Bernachon chocolates from Lyons, France, were once the exclusive import of Takashimaya, and it was worth a special trip to this department store just to buy them. Unfortunately, they are no longer sold here (nor anywhere else in the U.S.). Now a French chocolatier makes the private-label truffles and assorted chocolates for the store. The terrific American-made Burdick chocolates (see page 16) are a recent addition. Holidays are occasions for special Burdick treats like the nut-studded chocolate egg with tiny truffles inside, available only at Easter time.

The gift boxes of tiny M&M-style chocolates come from Japan exquisitely packaged in papier-mâché containers resembling miniature vegetables. Sweets lovers be warned: Japanese chocolate is considerably more bitter than its Western counterpart. Expect to pay caviar prices for these morsels.

Chocolate Cakes, Cookies, and Brownies

For the chocolate lover, there are very few shopping experiences as rewarding as a visit to a pastry shop, particularly in New York, where chocolate baked goods are typically the biggest sellers at the city's best bakeries. With the shelves and counters lined with freshly baked beauties, it's often difficult to choose just one from among so many tempting treats. But when you finally walk away with that little white bag or big box tied up with a ribbon, you know that you're in for one of life's simple pleasures.

New York has such an abundance of great bakeshops that it isn't easy deciding which type to visit. Elegant or homey? French, Italian, German, Austrian, or all-American? A decades-old place or a trendy new shop? Maybe a place with cafe seating where you can enjoy a brownie with a cup of tea or coffee? Whatever your preference, you'll find it in New York.

France unquestionably has a rich history in the art of pastry making; we are fortunate, however, that talented expatriates have opened lovely patisseries throughout our city. We can have a buttery pain au chocolat in the morning or a slice of chocolate ganache cake in the afternoon to rival those found along the streets of Paris.

New York is also home to numerous ambitious young Americans who have put their own distinctive signatures on the classics, or created new desserts that have garnered their own cult following. These passionate professionals have put their time, money, and energy into opening new businesses, the result being that we can enjoy an ever-growing repertoire of wonderful chocolate desserts, from layer cakes and cupcakes to mousse pies, cheesecakes, and puddings.

Around town you can find delicate little chocolate cookies that seem to melt in your mouth, and jumbo chocolate chip cookies nearly as big as Frisbees, that will help you get through a tough day. There are countless versions of that American classic, the brownie. Choose your weapon: moist and dense or cakey and light; studded with chocolate bits or nuts, or maybe both.

And this being New York, you can find more unusual offerings, like a lavishly decorated chocolate cake as tall as Patrick Ewing (and costing as much as a new car), or a shop dedicated to guilt-free, reduced-fat baked goods. We can have our cake and eat it too!

Andrew's Bakery and Chocolate Factory

61 New Dorp Plaza, Staten Island 718-667-9696
Hours: Wednesday through Saturday 7:00 a.m. to 6:00 p.m.,
Sunday 7:00 a.m. to 5:00 p.m.
Prices: Moderate; No Credit Cards

THIS GERMAN-AMERICAN BAKERY has been thrilling Staten Island residents for close to 20 years. Sundays are the busiest days, when a buy-one-get-one-free offer stands. The line grows so long that the owners often have to set up a canopy for people to stand under. Free coffee and samples add to the festivity.

The chocolate mousse cake and Black Forest cake are great, and birthday cakes are a big specialty. They also make their own chocolate candies and terrific dipped fruits—strawberries, pineapple, and cherries.

Service is extremely helpful at Andrew's; they even carry big boxes out to customers' cars. The bakery shuts down every

Fourth of July and reopens around Labor Day. Before it closes, the owners throw a big party for neighborhood children, complete with clowns, face painting, and kiddie rides.

Black Forest Pastry Shop

177 First Ave. at 11th St.   254-8181
Hours: Monday through Saturday 8:00 a.m.
to 8:00 p.m.; Sunday 9:30 a.m. to 5:30 p.m.
Prices: Moderate; No Credit Cards

IT IS NOT OFTEN THAT YOU CAN WALK into a bakery and be rewarded with free samples of chocolate truffles. But that is exactly what happened to us at this modest little place owned by a baker born in Heidelberg, Germany. "He is also part Austrian," said the counterwoman and supplier of the free samples. She added, "It's why the chocolate desserts are so good." And they are, with a rustic, homemade look about them.

The best-sellers are the Sacher torte, sold whole or by the slice, and, of course, the Black Forest cake, a delicious whipped cream–topped cake with kirsch-laced cherries and hunks of chocolate. Wow.

Black Forest also makes rum truffles that really pack a wallop, and an interesting single-serving chocolate-covered coconut cake called a Mount Saint Helena. We saw the latter ordered by a neighborhood regular who couldn't resist digging in right away as he happily left the shop.

Black Hound

149 First Ave. at 9th St.   979-9505   (800) 344-4417
Hours: Monday through Friday Noon to 8:00 p.m.;
Saturday Noon to 7:00 p.m.; Sunday Noon to 6:00 p.m.
Prices: Expensive
Mail Order and Delivery Available: Call (800) 344-4417
Monday through Friday 9:00 a.m. to 5:00 p.m.

AS YOU STEP INSIDE THIS NARROW, half-sized store, you are instantly transported from the streets of Manhattan to a sophisticated country atmosphere complete with sloping wide-board floors and antique pine cabinets displaying tempting sweets.

The triple mousse cake is justifiably the number one dessert seller. Layers of white, milk, and dark chocolate mousse rest on a thin piece of hazelnut cake, and bittersweet ganache coats the top. It's simple, luscious, and light.

Individual "ball" treats are fun and delicious: The Mud Ball is chocolate butter cake with chocolate buttercream covered with chocolate crumbs; the Snow Ball is chocolate butter cake with white chocolate buttercream covered with lightly roasted almonds. Try the delicate cookies made with premium Belgian bittersweet chocolate and a touch of black pepper. You'll get a pleasant hint of heat when you finish the last bite.

Handmade bittersweet truffles are the super-soft variety that melt almost the moment your fingers touch them. They are sold loose or in handsome wood Shaker boxes. For the ultimate chocolate gift, you might want to consider the handwoven chocolate basket brimming with an assortment of truffles. A favorite flavor is the Grand Marnier.

All of Black Hound's delicacies are made in Williamsburg, Brooklyn. Some of the desserts are sold at high-end food shops in Manhattan such as Balducci's and Grace's Marketplace.

Bonté Patisserie

1316 Third Ave. bet. 75th and 76th Sts.   535-2360
Hours: Monday through Saturday 9:00 a.m. to 6:30 p.m.
Prices: Expensive; No Credit Cards

THIS UPPER EAST SIDE FRENCH PATISSERIE does not look as if it has changed one bit since it opened more than two decades ago. It is still owned and run by the same married couple who came here from France. If classic French chocolate desserts are what you crave, this is your kind of place.

They make an attractive chocolate charlotte cake with chocolate mousse surrounded by ladyfingers, a chocolate sponge cake with raspberry and chocolate ganache, an elegant bittersweet flourless chocolate cake, and handmade truffles.

The pain au chocolat, a croissant filled with melted chocolate, is an irresistible treat along with a steaming cup of coffee. A favorite of ours is the chocolate Biarritz cookies, named after the seaside town in southwestern France where chocolate is very much revered.

CBK Cookies

226 E. 83rd St. bet. Second and Third Aves.   794-3383
366 Amsterdam Ave. bet. 77th and 78th Sts.   787-7702
Hours: Monday through Saturday 10:00 a.m. to 7:00 p.m.
(both locations)
Prices: Moderate
Mail Order and Delivery Available

SOME OF THE PRETTIEST AND TASTIEST COOKIES around town can be found at the pair of CBK shops—the windowed-kitchen Upper East Side store, where everything is baked, and the postage stamp–sized boutique on the Upper West Side. Charming collections of cookie jars decorate both locations.

Most of the cookies are the dainty variety, like the thin, square chocolate pecan wafers, which have barely a touch of sweetness. Other toothsome treats include chocolate hazelnut cookies, chocolate praline cookies, and mint juleps that are dipped in chocolate. Don't miss the yummy chocolate chip cookies.

Besides cookies, there are truffles, slivered almonds rolled in milk chocolate, chocolate cupcakes, and rich brownies studded with chocolate chips. Pleasant, professional sales help adds to the enjoyment of shopping at CBK.

Ceci-Cela Pâtisserie

55 Spring St. bet. Lafayette and Mulberry Sts.   274-9179
Hours: Monday through Saturday 7:00 a.m. to 7:00 p.m.
Prices: Moderate; No Credit Cards
Delivery Available
Cafe Seating

IF YOU'RE WANDERING THE STREETS of SoHo wishing you were on a rue somewhere in Paris, then head straight for Ceci-Cela on Spring Street. Patrons of this tiny shop breeze in and out, greeting owner and manager Herve Grall with a friendly "Bonjour," while co-owner and pastry chef Laurent Dupal creates his awesome treats in the kitchen downstairs.

In the morning you can't go wrong with the delicious almond pain au chocolat. It's baked twice, resulting in a crunchy, rich treasure.

Dupal loves truffles and makes a big batch every day. Amazingly priced at three for a dollar, these soft, fresh, intensely flavored balls move quickly. They are also the inspiration for Ceci-Cela's most popular dessert, the truffle cake—three layers of chocolate génoise that have been splashed with a bit of rum, filled with two layers of chocolate mousseline, coated with chocolate ganache, and topped with truffles. Amazingly, the cake is light. Available whole or by the slice, it alone is worth a trip to Spring Street.

The partners recently added a small salon in the back where you can enjoy a pastry and coffee and imagine, if only for a moment, that you're on the Left Bank.

The City Bakery

22 E.17th St. bet. Broadway and Fifth Ave. 366-1414
Hours: Monday through Saturday 7:30 a.m to 6:00 p.m.
Prices: Expensive
Delivery Available
Cafe Seating

THE CITY BAKERY, with its modern, minimalist decor, is a favorite destination for the downtown crowd. Regulars like to settle in to savor the light meals and the sophisticated baked goods meticulously prepared under the supervision of chef-owner Maury Rubin.

The tarts are Rubin's claim to fame. Each of these delicious creations looks like a work of contemporary art. There's a white chocolate cream tart in a chocolate pastry, and a wonderful silky rich chocolate cream tart. The chocolate mousse cake is a real crowd pleaser.

Hot chocolate, too, is taken very seriously at City Bakery, where it's made with melted French chocolate, cream, whole milk, and skim milk, although Rubin keeps the exact formula a secret. Every February, the bakery hosts a hot chocolate festival where you can choose from an eclectic array of infused flavors such as banana, chili pepper, citrus, and vanilla.

Cupcake Café

522 Ninth Ave. at 39th St.   465-1530
Hours: Monday through Friday 7:00 a.m. to 7:30 p.m.;
Saturday 8:00 a.m. to 6:00 p.m.; Sunday 9:00 a.m. to 5:00 p.m.
Prices: Moderate to Expensive; No Credit Cards
Cafe Seating

THIS FUNKY AND FUN 1950ish bakery and lunch stop makes the best chocolate buttercream in town—wickedly rich and smooth without being overly sweet. It is sensational atop their homemade-tasting layer cake. We like it best combined with the vanilla cake. Don't miss out on the terrific, moist chocolate cake, usually paired with vanilla buttercream. But nobody will stop you from ordering the double: a chocolate buttercream–chocolate cake combination.

Baker and co-owner Ann Warren has a talent for decorating everything she creates—from the tiny junior cupcakes to that special-occasion birthday cake. Her floral decorations are bursts of yellow, red, green, and even purple buttercreams. They are works of art and look almost too pretty to eat.

Brownies and Toll House chocolate chip cookies round out the list of items here for the chocolate lover. Both the cupcakes and the cakes with the magnificent floral designs can be found in some of the big-name food emporiums around town.

Desserts by David Glass

Mail Order from mid-October to early March: (860) 525-0345;
(800) DAVID-99
Prices: Expensive

SERIOUS CHOCOHOLICS won't be disappointed with any of the products created by David Glass. The Ultimate Chocolate Truffle Cake is a dark and very intense flourless cake that will satisfy a deep-rooted chocolate craving.

There is also an all-natural, less-fat version that is sinfully rich, just like the original. It is ideal for anyone who is prone to bingeing on chocolate cake. Both cakes can be purchased by mail order, or they can be picked up at Balducci's in Greenwich Village, Zabar's on the Upper West Side, and Gourmet Garage in SoHo.

Duane Park Patisserie

179 Duane St. bet. Hudson and Greenwich Sts.   274-8447
Hours: Tuesday through Saturday 8:00 a.m. to 6:30 p.m.;
Sunday 9:00 a.m. to 5:00 p.m.
Prices: Moderate; No Credit Cards
Mail Order and Delivery Available
Cafe Seating

LOCATED IN AN INDUSTRIAL SECTION OF TRIBECA, where the loading docks fill up with trucks picking up butter and cream, is the Duane Park Patisserie, the retail arm of a wholesale business. It can sometimes be a difficult place to find, especially if the sidewalk sign is not in its usual spot. Inside, a nostalgic Formica kitchen counter with a few stools invites you to sit and enjoy a pain au chocolat in the morning or possibly a delicious chunky brownie on a lazy afternoon.

A good bet here is the Sacher torte — chocolate sponge cake filled with apricot jam and covered with a chocolate icing. And do try the swirl-top chocolate cupcakes with the white filling. They remind us of the chocolate Hostess cupcakes — only far superior — that we took to school in our lunch pails as kids.

Egidio Pastry Shop

622 E. 187th St. bet. Hughes and Arthur Aves., Bronx
(718) 295-6077
Hours: Daily 7:00 a.m. to 8:00 p.m.
Prices: Moderate; No Credit Cards
Cafe Seating

A VISIT TO THE BELMONT SECTION OF THE BRONX is one of our favorite food excursions in all of New York. We love to go on a Saturday morning, when the best stores along Arthur Avenue and 187th Street are bustling with neighborhood residents and are at their liveliest.

A trip to Belmont would not be complete, however, without a stop at Egidio, where we might buy something to go, or perhaps settle down at one of the tables for cappuccino and a pastry.

Egidio's cannolis are among the best in New York. When you visit here, try the cannoli that's dipped in bittersweet

chocolate, a variation of the traditional Sicilian pastry that origi-
nated at Egidio. They also sell a good chocolate ring cake, which
is a moist chocolate sponge cake topped with a very sweet fudge
icing. Egidio sells so many of them that at peak times they bake
a fresh batch every two hours. The butter cookies, many of them
dipped in chocolate, are terrific. You'll regret it if you don't buy
an assortment to go.

From May through September, Egidio makes its own rum-
laced chocolate ice, a good, refreshing treat on a hot summer
day.

Houghtaling Mousse Pie Ltd.

389 Broome St. bet. Mulberry and Centre Sts.   226-3724
Hours: Monday through Thursday 9:00 a.m. to 7:00 p.m.;
Friday and Saturday Noon to 9:00 p.m.
Prices: Moderate; No Credit Cards
Mail Order and Delivery Available

SUE HOUGHTALING has been making her famous chocolate
mousse pies for almost two decades, many of them going to top
restaurants like Peter Luger Steak House in Brooklyn. But you
can buy them too, at very reasonable prices, from this shop that
borders Little Italy and SoHo.

The mousse is light, with just the right amount of chocolate richness, and the chocolate-nut crust is the perfect complement. Among other varieties of these pies, the chocolate and raspberry with chocolate crust is another good bet. The chocolate mousse itself is available in a pint-sized container. There are denser-style "truffle" pies, but the mousse pies are the real attraction here. Special decorating is available.

Hungarian Rigo Bakery

318 E. 78th St. bet. First and Second Aves.   988-0052
Hours: Monday 8:00 a.m. to 4:00 p.m.; Tuesday through Saturday
8:00 a.m. to 6:00 p.m.; Sunday 9:00 a.m. to 4:00 p.m.
Prices: Moderate; No Credit Cards

THIS DECADES-OLD EASTERN EUROPEAN BAKERY, situated on a quiet residential block in the Yorkville section of the Upper East Side, is one of the last of its kind. It has a sleepy look about it from the outside, and a real old-fashioned feel on the inside. There is a refrigerated case brimming with treats for the chocolate lover. They are made, according to the Transylvanian-born owner, by three homegrown Hungarian bakers. All items can be bought in individual serving sizes, and the chocolate mousse cake and the dobos (seven-layer) cake, both of which are very attractive, can be purchased whole in various sizes. The good dobos cake is available with either hardened caramel or chocolate fudge icing on top. Both versions have a rich chocolate buttercream filling that is silky and smooth.

Our favorite treat at Rigo is called the Chocolate Hazelnut Mountain, a combination of chopped hazelnuts and cake swirled inside a thin layer of chocolate. It looks like the top of a soft ice-cream cone that was dipped in chocolate sauce.

The chocolate mousse cake is good, but a bit sweet. Serve it with a strong Viennese coffee, and it will be fine.

Leske's Danish Bakery

7612 Fifth Ave. bet. 76th and 77th Sts., Brooklyn   (718) 680-2323
Hours: Tuesday through Saturday 6:00 a.m. to 6:30 p.m.;
Saturday 6:00 a.m. to 6:00 p.m.; Sunday 6:00 a.m. to 2:00 p.m.
Prices: Moderate; No Credit Cards

IF THERE IS ONE PLACE that all residents of the Bay Ridge section of Brooklyn know, it is Leske's. This landmark neighborhood bakery of Scandinavian heritage has been making fabulous Danish pastry for more than 80 years. Their chocolate treats, such as a dynamite chocolate-glazed doughnut with a yummy Boston cream filling, are also mighty popular.

Do you remember those giant black-and-white cookies, which seem to get harder and harder to find? Well, Leske's makes one of the best we've ever tasted. The fluffy, sweet icing over the cupcake-like bottom is perfection.

If chocolate seven-layer cake is your weakness, you must try the one made at Leske's; it is shaped like a brick and has a cherry on top. The light-as-a-feather chocolate layer cake topped with hard icing has a single, thick middle layer of the same chocolate buttercream as the seven-layer. They also make a similar cake with a soft fudge icing.

If you can't resist the Danish pastry counter, do try the custard kringler that is shaped like a giant pretzel. It has a touch of melted chocolate on top and is sprinkled with slivered almonds. It's delicious.

Leske's light, cakey brownies have a smattering of chopped walnuts inside and creamy fudge icing on top. The bottom is sugarcoated, which gives the brownie a nice feel when you bite into it. Have a few put into a separate wax bag so you can snack on them during the ride home.

Lipstick Cafe

885 Third Ave. at 54th St.   486-8664

Hours: Monday through Friday 11:30 a.m.

to 3:00 p.m. (table service until 2:30 p.m.)

Prices: Moderate; Cafe Seating

LOCATED IN THE LOBBY of the lipstick-shaped midtown office building, this cafe, owned by chef Jean-Georges Vongerichten of Jo Jo and Vong restaurant fame, operates as a lunch outpost for both table service and take-out. Although the menu changes with the seasons, two regular, outstanding chocolate offerings are an intense miniature chocolate tart and a delicious brownie studded with walnuts and chocolate chips. Both desserts are made with premium Valrhona chocolate and come with ice cream on the side. The brownie here gets our vote for the best in New York. Don't miss it!

∼LIPSTICK CAFE BROWNIE∼

Pastry chef Serge DeCrauzat is the creator of many of the wonderful desserts that are served at the Lipstick Cafe and the Jo Jo and Vong restaurants. We think his brownie, which can be bought at the Lipstick Cafe, is the best in New York. It's wonderfully rich, so a small piece goes a long way. These brownies are only about one-inch high. DeCrauzat uses only

---

premium extra-bittersweet Valrhona chocolate in his version.

12 ounces bittersweet chocolate, extract broken into pieces

$^{1}/_{2}$ pound (2 sticks) unsalted butter

1 cup sugar

3 eggs, lightly beaten

1 teaspoon vanilla

$^{1}/_{2}$ cup cake flour

$^{1}/_{2}$ teaspoon salt

1 $^{1}/_{2}$ cups walnuts

1 $^{1}/_{2}$ cups chocolate chips

1. Preheat the oven to 350°F. Lightly butter a rectangular cake pan (approximately 9" x 13") and set aside.

2. Place the chocolate in the top pot of a double boiler. Bring the water to a simmer and melt the chocolate over medium heat, stirring constantly with a wooden spoon.

3. In a mixing bowl, cream the butter with the sugar. Slowly add the eggs, then the vanilla extract. Fold in the cake flour, salt, and baking powder. Add the melted chocolate, walnuts, and chocolate chips, and gently stir to blend.

4. Pour the batter into the baking pan and smooth the top with a spatula. Bake for 30 minutes or until the top starts to crack and the cake has separated slightly from the side of the pan. Place the pan on a wire rack and cool completely before cutting the cake into squares.

Yields 12 brownies.

Madison Avenue's Better Baker

1006 Madison Ave. bet. 77th and 78th Sts.   396-0001

Toll-Free (888) Better-5

Hours: Monday through Friday 8:00 a.m. to 8:00 p.m.;

Saturday and Sunday 9:00 a.m. to 7:00 p.m.

Prices: Expensive

Delivery Available

Cafe Seating

WE ARE NOT USUALLY ones to seek out low-fat chocolate baked goods. There are fundamental laws of the dessert world that are too precious to tamper with.

Madison Avenue is, however, always up to something, and to cater to the increasing number of health-conscious people these days, the Better Baker opened last year with a reduced-fat theme.

They list the fat grams and calories of every product they make, which is great for anyone who is counting calories but can't live another moment without having a chocolate something or other.

Popular items include brownies, chocolate cupcakes, chocolate pound loaves, devil's food cake, chocolate mousse cups, and a rich-tasting cake called Chocolate Decadence. Add to this the catchy-named Cin-Free Choco-Berry Cake—our favorite reduced-fat goodie—and you have found yourself a niche in the dessert world.

Marquet Pâtisserie

15 E. 12th St. bet. University Pl. and Fifth Ave.   229-9313
Hours: Monday through Friday 7:30 a.m. to 8:00 p.m.;
Saturday 8:00 a.m. to 8:00 p.m.
Prices: Expensive; No Credit Cards
Delivery Available
Cafe Seating

WHAT STARTED OUT AS A TINY, country-style patisserie over
in Brooklyn has since moved to Greenwich Village and grown
into a Parisian-style cafe. Owner Jean-Pierre Marquet is the
chef, and his wife, Lynne Guillot, runs the day-to-day opera-
tions. Besides tables for light meals and coffee, there's take-out
and local delivery service.

You can purchase a good, sturdy hot chocolate, made with
melted chocolate instead of a mix, to sip as you ponder what
type of cake to take home.

The Marquise cake, made with smooth, silky chocolate
mousse covered with a thin robing of bittersweet chocolate, is a
sure bet, and the elegant Opera cake has a finesse that is hard
to find outside of Paris. Their pain au chocolat has always been
one of the contenders for the best in New York. A new addition
is homemade chocolate truffles, including ones laced with
Grand Marnier.

The baking for Marquet is still done in the original

Brooklyn patisserie, which has, regrettably, been turned into one huge kitchen.

Once Upon a Tart

135 Sullivan St. bet. Houston and Prince Sts.   387-8869
Hours: Monday through Friday 8:00 a.m. to 8:00 p.m.;
Saturday 9:00 a.m. to 8:00 p.m.; Sunday 9:00 a.m. to 6:00 p.m.
Prices: Moderate; No Credit Cards
Delivery Available
Cafe Seating

JERÔME AUDUREAU has brought the sunshine of his native Provence to SoHo. Ten years ago he left his hometown of Avignon, France, and landed in New York, ready to embark on his American career in hotel management. While working in that profession, he befriended colleague Frank Mentesana, a New Jersey native. In the fall of 1992, with a dream and a few cookbooks in hand, the two became partners and opened up a charming little take-out food shop in SoHo, specializing in sweet and savory tarts of all kinds. Word spread and the business grew, enabling the pair to lease an adjacent space a few years later and turn it into a small cafe.

Once Upon a Tart is now a lively spot with an appealing array of prepared foods and desserts. Chocolate lovers will surely find something pleasing among the sweet selections. Try the brownie, which is moist and not too dense. Among the very good scones is a version flavored with orange and bits of chocolate. Other treats include chocolate chip cookies, crunchy chocolate walnut macaroons, chocolate walnut tarts, chocolate hazelnut biscotti, and rich cups of hot chocolate.

∼ Once Upon a Tart's Chocolate Chip Cookies ∼

$3/4$ cup (1 $1/2$ sticks) butter, at room temperature

1 $1/2$ cups brown sugar

1 egg

1 teaspoon vanilla extract

2 $1/4$ cups flour, sifted

1 teaspoon baking powder

$1/4$ teaspoon salt

1 $1/2$ cups bittersweet chocolate chips

1. Preheat the oven to 375°F.

2. With an electric mixer, cream the butter until very creamy.

3. Mix in the brown sugar.

4. Mix in the egg and vanilla.

5. Gradually add the flour, baking powder, and salt and mix until well combined.

6. Stir in the chocolate chips.

7. Drop tablespoonfuls of the batter about two inches apart on Teflon cookie sheets. Bake for about 8 to 9 minutes, or until the tops are lightly browned.

Yields about 4 dozen cookies.

Oxford Bake Shop

104-01 Liberty Ave. at 104th St., Ozone Park, Queens

(718) 843-4039

Hours: Tuesday through Sunday 6:00 a.m. to 7:00 p.m.

Prices: Inexpensive; No Credit Cards

FOR A TASTY TRIP BACK IN TIME, catch the next A train bound for Lefferts Boulevard. When the train emerges from the tunnel, there are only four outdoor stations standing between you and truly wonderful chocolate desserts. Jump off at the 104th Street/Oxford Avenue stop, hurry down the elevated steps, and right there you will find the Oxford Bake Shop, a neighborhood landmark for more than 50 years.

Inside, you'll see how the extra-long marble counter and the wood and glass shelves have gracefully aged. They are the perfect showcase for the classic baked goods, which are honest and pure, and always have a just-baked freshness to them.

The devil's food cake here is second to none. Try the Continental version, a delicious layer cake with chocolate whipped-cream filling and dark chocolate fudge on top. You'll find it in the refrigerated section along with another marvel—the Blackout—the same devil's food but with chocolate pudding between the layers and topped with a coating of chocolate crumbs.

The traditional layer cakes are also very good. Not too dense, not too gooey, but just right. Layers of devil's food cake or vanilla cake are interspersed with layers of chocolate butter-cream and covered in chocolate fudge. A combination called the Checkerboard consists of alternating squares of the devil's food and vanilla cakes lightly held together by chocolate butter-cream, with chocolate fudge icing coating the whole creation.

Other specialties include Black Forest cake, chocolate doughnuts, and chocolate French crullers.

And don't leave without an assortment of the butter cookies. Vanilla cookies, some filled with apricot preserves, are dipped in a lovely chocolate glaze. The chocolate butter cookies come in various combinations with or without the glaze, and some are filled with raspberry preserves. Try a few of each.

When the amiable clerk tells you your final tally, you may not believe your ears. The prices at Oxford are a throwback too.

Patisserie J. Lanciani

414 W. 14th St. bet. 9th Ave. and Washington St.   989-1213

Hours: Monday through Saturday 8:00 a.m. to 8:00 p.m.;

Sunday 9:00 a.m. to 8:00 p.m.

Prices: Expensive

Delivery Available

PATISSERIE J. LANCIANI moved in 1995 from a pretty Greenwich Village street to the West Side meatpacking district, redefining itself primarily as a wholesale business. A small shop was added in May 1996. Sadly, the cafe with the charming little tables was left behind at their old location.

Now, if you're willing to brave it, you'll need to make your way along this cobblestoned street where you'll see, attached to the buildings, those old steel roof racks that were once used to slide huge sides of beef onto awaiting tractor trailers.

Inside Patisserie J. Lanciani, there is just enough room to stand and peer down into the two glass counters filled with lovely chocolate cakes.

The old-fashioned layer cakes include a vanilla cake with a chocolate buttercream filling and chocolate crumb topping, and a fantastic devil's food cake with chocolate buttercream. Both cakes are sold whole or by the slice. There's also a heart-shaped chocolate mousse cup with whipped cream on top and a sliver of dark chocolate in the center. The rich, velvety mousse is perfectly complemented by its bittersweet chocolate container.

If you can't make it to this meatpacking street, you can always pick up your phone: For a $10 delivery charge, they'll bring dessert right to your door.

Patisserie Les Friandises

972 Lexington Ave. bet. 70th and 71st Sts.   988-1616
Hours: Monday through Saturday 8:00 a.m. to 7:00 p.m.;
Sunday 9:00 a.m. to 6:00 p.m.
Prices: Expensive; No Credit Cards
Delivery Available
Cafe Seating

CHOCOLATE IS GIVEN ITS DUE at this French-inspired bakeshop, located in a lovely area of the Upper East Side. The best-selling pastries are the chocolate mousse cake and the meringue boule, which is chocolate meringue dipped in chocolate, filled with bittersweet chocolate and orange ganache, and topped with meringue chips. Boxes can be filled to order with cake or an assortment of chocolate confections.

Their hot chocolate mix once came from the famous Angelina of Paris, but now Les Friandises serves hot chocolate made from their own recipe. Something chilled and chocolate is sold during the summer, be it a cool drink, granita, or sorbet.

Sant Ambroeus

1000 Madison Ave. bet. 77th and 78th Sts.   570-2211

Hours: Monday through Saturday 9:30 a.m. to 10:30 p.m.;

Sunday 10:30 a.m. to 6:00 p.m.

Prices: Very Expensive

Delivery Available

Cafe Seating

THERE IS NO PLACE IN NEW YORK that reminds us more of the cafes of Milan than Sant Ambroeus. As in those found in the business and fashion capital of Italy, the service here is attentive, the prices are expensive, and closing hours are late every evening (except Sunday).

The next time you're in this neighborhood, stop in for a piece of chocolate cake. Sant Ambroeus will sell you a slice of any of the cakes in their impressive selection. Ask for it to stay, and they will graciously serve it on a plate. Do take it over to the bar (as they do in Italy) to enjoy it with the best cup of cappuccino in the city. Or if you prefer, you can patronize the ristorante in the rear of the shop.

The rich and flavorful chocolate cake topped with fresh orange slices is particularly good. There's also a small selection of chocolate-filled candies and truffles. In the cooler months, you'll find fresh gooseberries covered in chocolate. The still-attached leaves make ideal handles.

The gelato at Sant Ambroeus is terrific. The creamy chocolate-hazelnut is a rich and satisfying choice, with the chocolate chip a very close second.

Sarabeth's Kitchen

423 Amsterdam Ave. bet. 80th and 81st Sts.   496-6280

1295 Madison Ave. bet. 92nd and 93rd Sts.   410-7335

Hours: Monday through Friday 8:00 a.m. to 11:00 p.m.;

Saturday 9:00 a.m. to 11:00 p.m.; Sunday 9:00 a.m. to 10:00 p.m.

Closed daily from 5:00 p.m. to 6:00 p.m.

Prices: Very Expensive

Cafe Seating

BOTH LOCATIONS OF SARABETH'S KITCHEN have bakery counters where chocolate treats await your pleasure. On the menu and available for take-out are brownies and a trio of chocolate cakes — soufflé, mousse, and truffle; all good and fresh, but the small pieces carry somewhat high prices. We also like the chubbie, a double chocolate chip-walnut cookie that is cakelike inside.

Thankfully, Sarabeth's usually sells a wonderful, creamy, homemade chocolate pudding, a comforting treat that is increasingly hard to find in this city. It is topped with a dollop of whipped cream and chocolate shavings. For take-out it comes in a preserves jar, which requires a 50-cent deposit that is refunded on return of the jar. NOTE: There is a Sarabeth's at the Whitney Museum, for eating in only.

Soutine

104 W. 70th St. bet. Columbus Ave. and Broadway   496-1450
Hours: Monday through Friday 8:00 a.m. to 7:00 p.m.;
Saturday 9:00 a.m. to 5:00 p.m.; Sunday 9:00 a.m. to 3:00 p.m.
Prices: Expensive; No Credit Cards
Mail Order and Delivery Available

AT THIS MINUSCULE SHOP you can buy a cake called a Chocolate Concorde that is made with a delightful combination of chocolate mousse and chocolate meringue topped with long, thin meringue curls. It is light and airy, in contrast to the sturdy flourless and dense chocolate cake that is also popular here.

Who wouldn't be thrilled with a chocolate cake delivered right to their door? Soutine can add fanfare to a long-distance birthday celebration. They will gladly decorate a cake with a personal message and ship it anywhere in the United States. The owners told us that when it comes to birthday cakes, their chocolate variety leads all others by a margin of four to one.

Chocolate truffles are frequently sold here, but a special order is recommended to guarantee availability.

Sylvia Weinstock Cakes Ltd.

273 Church St. bet. Franklin and White Sts.   925-6698
Hours: By Appointment Only
Prices: Very Expensive; No Credit Cards
Delivery Available

SYLVIA WEINSTOCK, the dessert doyenne of society parties, makes special-event cakes like no other. The drama of a Weinstock creation is topped only by its price. Her smallest, simplest (but by no means plain) cakes start at $350, and some of her fabulous wedding cakes can run as high as five figures.

The walls of Weinstock's office are lined with photos of public figures, celebrities, and the super-rich, all with dazzling smiles, cutting into her masterpieces. She personally tends to all new orders, encouraging clients to try the samples available that day. Who can resist as the heavenly aroma of just-baked cakes drifts in from the adjacent kitchen?

Most of the creations are painstakingly decorated with exquisite, lifelike edible flowers made of sugar. Unlike some fancy cakes, a Weinstock cake tastes as good as it looks. The moist chocolate cake, made with Belgian chocolate, is justifiably the biggest seller, and for a doubly delicious chocolate experience, it can be filled with a lovely, light chocolate mousse.

Taylor's

523 Hudson St. bet. W. 10th and Charles Sts.   645-8200
Hours: Monday through Friday 6:00 a.m. to 10:00 p.m.;
Saturday and Sunday 7:00 a.m. to 10:00 p.m.

228 W. 18th St. bet. Seventh and Eighth Aves.   366-9081
Hours: Monday through Friday 6:00 a.m. to 8:00 p.m.;
Saturday and Sunday 7:00 a.m. to 7:00 p.m.

175 Second Ave. bet. 11th and 12th Sts.   674-9501
Hours: Monday through Thursday and Sunday 7:00 a.m.
to 11:00 p.m.; Friday and Saturday 7:00 a.m. to Midnight
Prices: Moderate; No Credit Cards

IF YOU ARE LOOKING for a little country charm to go along
with your chocolate fix, visit the original store on Hudson
Street. With its old-fashioned windowpanes and tiny picket
fence, you'll feel like you're stepping into a picture-postcard
storefront in a New England town.

If you decide on a brownie, the pleasant and folksy people
behind the counter of this cramped shop will invite you to
reach over and select your own from the big stack in the front
window. The brownies are robust and dense. One variety, the
Zebra, comes with a layer of cheesecake on top, so you can satisfy two different cravings at once.

Taylor's is best known for their marvelous chocolate fallen soufflé cake, available in a number of different sizes. Chocolate mavens head to Taylor's for this one.

There are three benches out on the sidewalk, where you can relax in the sun and enjoy an oversized chocolate chip cookie. Get to Taylor's in the morning for the best selection.

Both the Chelsea and East Village branches carry the same homey desserts.

Trois Jean

154 E. 79th St. bet. Lexington and Third Aves.   988-4858
Hours: Monday through Saturday 11:00 a.m. to 11:00 p.m.;
Sunday 11:00 a.m. to 10:00 p.m.
Prices: Expensive
Cafe Seating

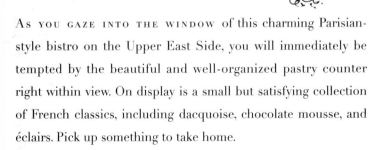

As you gaze into the window of this charming Parisian-style bistro on the Upper East Side, you will immediately be tempted by the beautiful and well-organized pastry counter right within view. On display is a small but satisfying collection of French classics, including dacquoise, chocolate mousse, and éclairs. Pick up something to take home.

The dessert specialty is called a Pyramide au Chocolat. It is made of a satisfyingly smooth ganache consisting of three kinds of imported chocolate and shaped into a pyramid. This good-looking and good-tasting treat comes in a few sizes.

William Greenberg Jr. Desserts

1100 Madison Ave. bet. 82nd and 83rd Sts.   744-0304
Hours: Monday through Friday 9:00 a.m. to 6:30 p.m.;
Saturday 9:00 a.m. to 6:00 p.m.; Sunday 10:00 a.m. to 4:30 p.m.

2187 Broadway bet. 77th and 78th Sts.   580-7300
Hours: Monday through Friday 9:00 a.m. to 7:00 p.m.;
Saturday 9:00 a.m. to 6:00 p.m.; Sunday 10:00 a.m. to 4:30 p.m.

518 Third Ave. bet. 34th and 35th Sts.   686-3344*
Hours: Monday through Saturday 9:00 a.m. to 6:00 p.m.

60 E. 8th St. bet. Broadway and Mercer St.   995-9184*
Hours: Monday through Friday 7:30 a.m. to 7:00 p.m.;
Saturday 9:00 a.m. to 7:00 p.m.; Sunday 11:00 a.m. to 5:00 p.m.

459 Seventh Ave. bet 34th and 35th Sts. (Macy's)   494-1091*
Hours: Monday through Friday 7:30 a.m. to 8:00 p.m.;
Saturday 9:00 a.m. to 7:30 p.m.; Sunday 9:00 a.m. to 6:00 p.m.
Prices: Expensive; Delivery Available
*Cafe Seating

MORE THAN 50 YEARS AGO, William Greenberg Jr. sailed back to New York after serving in World War II. Up until then, Uncle Sam had been his only employer, and Greenberg found himself with no immediate plans for a career. A big night at the poker table changed that. With barely enough from his winnings, he opened his first bakery. Now there are William Greenberg Jr. Desserts scattered about the city. Although he recently sold the business, Greenberg can still be seen decorating cakes at the Madison Avenue shop.

Chocolate is paramount in the Greenberg repertoire, with nearly 20 kinds of chocolate cakes. We like the Candy Cake—thinly sliced bittersweet chocolate layers filled with whipped cream, covered in a chocolate ganache glaze, and garnished with chocolate wafers.

When we heard about the new cheesecake with a thick layer of chocolate mousse and a chocolate ganache glaze, we were admittedly a bit skeptical about such an ambitious combination. But after trying a small slice, we found ourselves going back for more!

The Greenberg cakes are good, fresh, and homey, and are ideal for those looking for a rich chocolate experience. Besides the cakes, you'll find terrific brownies and other treats like truffles and chocolate rugelach.

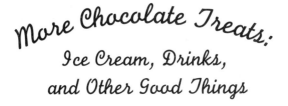

More Chocolate Treats:
Ice Cream, Drinks, and Other Good Things

As we traveled throughout New York's wonderful world of chocolate, we discovered the countless ways chocolate is used other than in candies and cakes.

More and more places have begun serving authentic hot chocolate, made with melted premium chocolate, milk, and cream. These steaming, rich cups help to make New York winters bearable. At any time of year, that New York classic, the chocolate egg cream, always hits the spot, although it's true that a really good version is becoming harder and harder to find.

As the sun beats down in the summer, chocolate can be enjoyed in its chilly form. We like to treat ourselves to an icy granita or a delicious scoop of ice cream. Or maybe we'll splurge and have a sundae topped with rich hot fudge and whipped cream. Sadly, many of the old-fashioned ice cream parlors with their counter service, soda fountains, and home-made chocolate lollipops are long gone. Perhaps none more noticeably than Rumpelmayer's, which has been reduced to nothing more than a hotel coffee shop. On the brighter side, there are new fun places that serve up great frozen treats.

Chocolate is even offered in unexpected ways. We found unusual but delicious creations by professionals who have brought a chocolate touch to everyday foods. Now we can go to a bread shop for lovely loaves of chocolate bread, or have heart-shaped chocolate butter delivered to our favorite chocolate lover. What will they think of next?

A.L. Bazzini Co.

339 Greenwich St. at Jay St.   334-1280; (800) 228-0172
Hours: Monday through Friday 8:00 a.m. to 7:00 p.m.;
Saturday 9:30 a.m. to 6:00 p.m.
Prices: Inexpensive
Mail Order Available

ONE OF THE BEST SOURCES FOR NUTS in New York is Bazzini's. Because the company does a large wholesale business, shoppers at the retail outpost in TriBeCa are rewarded with super-fresh products sold at extremely reasonable prices. Aware that chocolate and nuts are a match made in heaven, the Bazzini family offers a terrific selection of chocolate-covered nuts, from almonds, filberts, peanuts, and cashews to pecans and—our all-time favorite—walnuts.

They're all great with coffee at the end of a big dinner. Look for the one-pound cellophane bags. Just be careful to avoid the identical-looking but inferior-tasting carob-masquerading-as-chocolate-covered nuts. On a nearby shelf, bakers will find Merkens chocolate in one-pound chunks.

We only wish the service at Bazzini's were a little more helpful, but we return to Bazzini's again and again because their products are so good.

Caffe Mille Luci

7123 18th Ave. at 72nd St., Brooklyn   (718) 837-7017

Hours: Monday through Friday 6:30 a.m. to 2:00 a.m.;

Saturday 7:00 a.m. to 3:00 a.m.; Sunday 7:00 a.m. to Midnight

Prices: Expensive; No Credit Cards; Cafe Seating

LOCATED IN THE BENSONHURST SECTION OF BROOKLYN
on food-famous 18th Avenue, this modern cafe makes some of
the best homemade gelato we've tasted. We don't know what
their secret is, but everything we try here is always first-rate.
You'd have to go to Italy to find better.

The extraordinary chocolate flavors include basic chocolate,
chocolate-hazelnut, and their specialty, chocolate baci, which
contains bits of hazelnuts. The gelato is packed in various-sized
containers to go, or it can be enjoyed anytime at the cafe,
including well into the wee hours of the morning.

Ciao Bella Gelato

262 Mott St. bet. Houston and Prince Sts.   226-7668;
Mail Order (800) 343-5286
Hours: Monday through Friday 10:00 a.m. to 6:00 p.m.
Prices: Moderate; No Credit Cards, except for mail order

NEW YORK HAS A GREAT ICE CREAM to call its own. The Ciao Bella factory, a bright oasis on an otherwise unassuming strip on Mott Street, is where heavenly sorbetto and gelato are made. It's also the secret source of many desserts served by better restaurants in town.

You can buy pints upstairs at the factory throughout the year. During the summer, stop by the vividly painted archway of the street-level shop to order scoops and pint containers.

Try the intensely flavored chocolate sorbetto, or the lusciously creamy gelato in flavors like chocolate and chocolate-hazelnut. You can special-order the five-liter tubs that chefs buy, which we think are perfect for grand-scale home entertaining. Additional flavors in this jumbo size include Nero chocolate, which is double dark, and Valrhona chocolate, made with the premium French couverture.

Opening times at the retail shop fluctuate, so it's best to call ahead before you visit. When the weather's warm, you'll find a kiosk at Lincoln Center. And if you're in SoHo, look for the Ciao Bella stand at the southwest corner of Prince and Mercer Streets.

Pints of Ciao Bella can also be found at gourmet shops and fancy coffee bars around town. Call the factory number for a location near you.

The Comfort Diner

214 E. 45th St. bet. Second and Third Aves.   867-4555
Hours: Monday through Friday 7:00 a.m. to 10:00 p.m.;
Saturday 10:00 a.m. to 10:00 p.m.; Sunday 10:00 a.m. to 9:00 p.m.
Prices: Moderate
Table and Counter Seating

As we combed the city in search of all things chocolate, we began to fear that the classic New York chocolate egg cream had become extinct. Then we stumbled upon The Comfort Diner.

At this showcase re-creation of a 1940s-style diner, owner Ira Freehof makes the best egg cream in all of New York. He uses the traditional, well-known Fox's U-Bet Chocolate Syrup, and the seltzer comes right out of those old-fashioned bottles with the spray nozzle on top.

"Marvin the seltzer man from Staten Island delivers to us once a week," the owner told us proudly. "The truck pulls up loaded with big baby-blue seltzer bottles in those old wooden crates."

The traditional recipe for a chocolate egg cream calls for chocolate syrup first, followed by a touch of milk, and seltzer to finish. No eggs. The Comfort Diner, however, learned from Marvin that the key to a good foamy head is to add the seltzer *after* the milk, followed last by a gentle drizzle of U-Bet syrup. The result is a head that's a creamy wonder.

The Comfort Diner also serves up chocolate malteds and chocolate milk shakes, both of them rich and smooth. The owner's cousin from White Plains supplies the good, home-made-tasting ice cream.

Nevertheless, we will always relish our first sip of the oh-so-frothy egg cream, thanks to the advice of Marvin the seltzer man.

~ THE COMFORT DINER CHOCOLATE EGG CREAM ~

Every true New Yorker knows that the classic chocolate egg cream does not contain eggs. It is made with three basic ingredients: milk, seltzer, and chocolate syrup. The secret of a great egg cream — mixing the ingredients in the proper sequence to produce a white frothy head — comes from the folks at The Comfort Diner.

$\frac{1}{3}$ cup milk
$\frac{2}{3}$ cup seltzer

3 tablespoons Fox's U-Bet Chocolate Syrup,
   plus additional for serving

1. Pour the milk into a tall glass, then add the seltzer.
2. Slowly drizzle in the syrup while quickly stirring with a
long spoon.
3. Serve additional syrup on the side.

Serves 1

Ecce Panis

1120 Third Ave. bet. 65th and 66th Sts.   535-2099
Hours: Monday through Friday 8:00 a.m. to 8:00 p.m.;
Saturday and Sunday 8:00 a.m. to 6:00 p.m.

1260 Madison Ave. bet. 90th and 91st Sts.   348-0040
Hours: Monday through Friday 8:00 a.m. to 7:00 p.m.;
Saturday and Sunday 8:00 a.m. to 6:00 p.m.
Prices: Very Expensive
Mail Order Available

WHILE CHOCOLATE LOVERS may not ordinarily think of a
bread shop as the place for a fix, those who visit Ecce Panis will
be pleasantly surprised. The Tiffany's of bread shops, this store
bakes some of the best—and most beautiful—breads in Man-

hattan, among them a fine chocolate-flavored loaf studded with chunks of premium Valrhona chocolate. If you wish, you may buy just half of the one-pound loaf, which is available every Friday, Saturday, and Sunday. It makes a great weekend breakfast treat.

Cravings for chocolate can be further satisfied with topnotch chocolate macadamia and chocolate hazelnut biscotti, or with the fabulous jumbo cookies—either the regular chocolate chip or the chocolate chocolate chip, contenders for the best in town.

Egg Farm Dairy

2 John Walsh Blvd., Peekskill, N.Y.
Mail Order: (914) 734-7343; (800) CREAMERY
Prices: Moderate

THIS UPSTATE VENTURE, a partnership between cheese maker Jonathan White and New York chef Charlie Palmer, was established several years ago. "Setting the dairy industry back 100 years" is the company motto. Butter, for instance, is made in small batches—and the result is a deliciously creamy product. Here's the romantic twist: The Egg Farm Dairy produces a heart-shaped chocolate butter that is made by slowly mixing premium bittersweet chocolate into the sweet butter. It's great on toast, waffles, and pancakes. You can order it by mail, or find it at cheese stores and food emporiums around holidays.

Mr. Chips

27 E. 92nd St. bet. Fifth and Madison Aves.   831-5555
Hours: Daily 11:30 a.m. to 10:00 p.m.

200 W. 57th St. at Seventh Ave.   956-5555
Hours: Monday through Friday 8:00 a.m. to Midnight;
Saturday and Sunday Noon to Midnight
Prices: Moderate

THE FIRST MR. CHIPS ice cream parlor opened in the Carnegie Hill neighborhood a few years ago. It's a fun, colorful place to skate into for a cone (in-line skaters *are* welcome) or to sit and enjoy a decadent hot fudge sundae.

The ice cream, which is made in Pennsylvania, is one of the best scoops to be found around town. There are at least a half dozen varieties of chocolate, including the terrific triple-charged Chocolate Thunder — chocolate ice cream with chocolate chips and ribbons of fudge. And do try the creamy chocolate mousse.

A second branch of the store recently opened opposite Carnegie Hall. Music lovers with chocolate on their minds can cross Seventh Avenue at intermission and hit a high note with a Mr. Chips cone.

Moondog

378 Bleecker St. bet. Perry and Charles Sts.   675-4540
Hours: Monday through Thursday and Sunday 11:00 a.m.
to 11:00 p.m.; Friday and Saturday 11:00 a.m. to Midnight
Prices: Moderate to Expensive; No Credit Cards

MOONDOG IS A WELCOME ADDITION to the New York ice cream scene. Customers pile into this pint-sized shop, where twin stereo speakers play rock music that echoes off the original tin ceiling.

Take a minute to study the ever-changing selections on the blackboard. The ingenious flavors cater to the chocoholic in us all. Regular customers waiting in line will happily offer advice on what flavor to try. Good ice cream makes everyone more sociable.

Some specials have included chocolate-banana, milk chocolate, and Oreo cookie. Ask for a sample, and the counterman gladly reaches for a miniature throwaway spoon and loads it up.

Their basic chocolate ice cream is the dark and intense variety. Have it as is, or in either of two outrageous chocolate concoctions. One, called a Brownie Sundae, consists of a home-made brownie underneath the chocolate ice cream, all doused with hot fudge. The fudge sauce is velvety rich and served at the perfect temperature. Chocolate Hell is the name of the other house specialty. Here, Moondog's own version of a sinfully rich truffle cake is topped with the chocolate ice cream and hot fudge sauce. Go for it!

Besides their popular cones, Moondog makes ice cream cakes and offers half-pints, pints, and quarts of their homemade ice cream to take home. There are only three stools inside Moondog, plus a couple of two-seater benches out on the sidewalk. This is a get-in get-out ice cream parlor.

The Parlor at Café des Artistes

1 W. 67th St. bet. Central Park West and Columbus Ave.   579-2506
Hours: Monday through Friday 8:00 a.m. to Midnight;
Saturday 10:00 a.m. to Midnight; Sunday 10:00 a.m. to 11:00 p.m.
Prices: Very Expensive
Cafe Seating

THE PARLOR AT CAFÉ DES ARTISTES is a lovely, unique spot in Manhattan. It is located in the landmark Hotel des Artistes building, across the lobby from the famed restaurant of the same name.

The small room is inviting, with lead glass windows overlooking the tree-lined street, chocolate-colored walls, and old-world decor — including an antique zinc bar from Paris and several small marble tables. Overall, it has the feel of an exclusive, intimate club. It's an ideal respite from city life, a place to linger over something delicious.

You can order from a selection of desserts made at the restaurant. Our number one choice is the outrageous hot fudge sundae that you make yourself from a platter laden with all the necessary ingredients: a bowl with two scoops of creamy, custardy French vanilla ice cream; a smaller bowl with whipped cream; a tiny container of fresh chopped walnuts; and a bowl of the best hot fudge sauce we've ever had. It's rich, chocolatey, and just on the edge of sweetness. We still talk about it.

There are also good chocolate cakes. We like the chocolate-raspberry one. For a truly incredible chocolate dessert experience, come with a friend or loved one and order the Chocolatissimo for Two. This platter contains miniature servings of *seven* chocolate desserts! You'll think you've died and gone to chocolate heaven.

∼ Café des Artistes' Hot Fudge Sauce ∼

Chef Thomas Ferlesch was generous in sharing his recipe for the delicious hot fudge sauce that is served with the sundaes at the Parlor at Café des Artistes.

1 cup heavy cream

6 tablespoons unsalted butter

$^1/_2$ cup white sugar

$^3/_4$ cup dark brown sugar

2 $^1/_2$ ounces semisweet
  chocolate, broken into pieces

$^3/_4$ cup cocoa powder

1 ounce dark rum

  Splash of Amaretto
  liqueur (optional)

1. Heat the cream, butter, and both sugars over low heat just until the butter and sugar have melted.

2. Remove from the heat and add the chocolate and cocoa powder. Let the mixture sit for 15 minutes or until the chocolate is completely melted. Do not stir.

3. Mix with a whisk, then add the rum, and the Amaretto.

Makes approximately 2 cups.

The Petrossian Delicacies Shop

182 W. 58th St. at Seventh Ave. 245-2217

Hours: Monday through Friday 10:00 a.m. to 10:00 p.m.;

Saturday 10:00 a.m. to 8:00 p.m.; Sunday 10:00 a.m. to 6:00 p.m.

Prices: Very Expensive

Mail Order and Delivery Available

THE KING OF CAVIAR has paid homage to chocolate. Petrossian sells pearl-sized gems of dark chocolate filled with a splash of vodka. Packed in caviar tins, they are shipped regularly from Paris, but high demand can keep them missing from the shelves. You may have more luck finding the other flavors— cherry, cognac, mocha, and mint.

Perfect as the grand finale of a formal dinner, these pearls are divine and priced accordingly. Keep them in mind as a gift for your favorite host or hostess. You can pick them up at the boutique, which is located off the vestibule of the luxury Art Deco restaurant.

Ray's Candy Store

113 Avenue A.   No Phone
Hours: Daily 24 hours
Prices: Inexpensive; No Credit Cards

You don't come to Ray's if you're looking for neat and pretty. This is an old-time hole-in-the-wall candy store with its own special kind of charm. Ray's is located directly across the street from Tompkins Square Park and has a window counter opening onto the sidewalk, as no more than a dozen people can fit inside the place.

If you do venture inside, you are immediatly confronted by a giant wooden magazine rack that's brimming over. One sneeze and the monstrosity could fall down on your head. An arm's length to the right is the soda fountain, where that famous New York institution known as the egg cream is being kept alive. Neighborhood residents know that Ray's is where you can sample a good one.

So what if the egg cream is served in a plastic cup: It will set you back only 50 cents. Fortunately, the counterfolks understand how to mix them. They come ice-cold, with a really good frothy head.

The chocolate milk shakes are also worth trying. They are the light and airy kind, reminiscent of the ones we had as kids from the Mister Softee trucks that played their familiar jingle as they drove around the neighborhood.

Savarese Pastry Shop

5924 New Utrecht Ave. at 60th St., Brooklyn   (718) 438-7770
Hours: Daily Noon to 10:00 p.m. (summer months only)
Prices: Moderate; No Credit Cards

SAVARESE PASTRY SHOP is a popular Bensonhurst institution. Our favorites here are the delicious homemade frozen treats that are sold only during the summer months. March right past the entrance to the pastry shop and go a little way down the block to the side window, where you can order wonderfully refreshing chocolate sorbetto and delectably creamy gelato in flavors like chocolate and chocolate-hazelnut.

Serendipity 3

225 E. 60th St. bet. Second and Third Aves. 838-3531

Hours: Monday through Thursday and Sunday 11:30 a.m.
to Midnight; Friday 11:30 a.m. to 1:00 a.m.;
Saturday 11:30 a.m. to 2:00 a.m.

Prices: Expensive

Cafe Seating

IF YOU ARE LOOKING for a somewhat different kind of place
to take the kids, you must visit Serendipity 3, an old-fashioned,
one-of-a-kind New York ice cream parlor.

As you step down the stairs and into the brownstone storefront, be sure to take in all the striking Tiffany lamps hanging
from the ceiling—a colorful contrast to the parlor-white interi-
or. The kids will want to gaze at the numerous cases filled with
trinkets, sold in what is referred to as the General Store.

Youngsters usually love to sit upstairs so they can charge up
the spiral staircase leading to a room that recalls a turn-of-the-
century New Orleans drawing room.

Chocolate fanatics come to Serendipity 3 for the famous
frozen hot chocolate drink, served in a giant goblet and topped
with a mountain of whipped cream.

The hot fudge sundae is still our preference. This, too, is a
tower, but the hot fudge and chocolate ice cream will be more
suited to the real chocolate connoisseur. Grand desserts are

everywhere; a slice of chocolate fudge cake will easily feed three.

Serendipity 3 is that special kind of New York place where you can have a fun time with a group—perhaps one of the reasons tourists flock here. It is a classic East Side scene that is a little bit wicked and always a touch wacky. It belongs in a Woody Allen film.

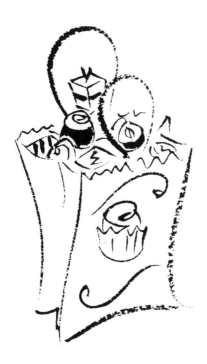

OTHER SOURCES FOR CHOCOLATE

ICE CREAM AND FROZEN TREATS

Agata & Valentina (page 52)

Egidio Pastry Shop (page 81)

Gourmet Garage (page 58)

Richart Design et Chocolat (page 37)

Sant Ambroeus (page 96)

OTHER SOURCES FOR HOT CHOCOLATE

The City Bakery (page 77)

Dean & DeLuca (page 54)

La Maison du Chocolat (page 27)

Marquet Pâtisserie (page 89)

Once Upon a Tart (page 90)

Patisserie Les Friandises (page 95)

Chocolate Making and Baking:
Supplies and Schools

Working with chocolate, be it making candy or baking a cake, is both an art and a science. Several schools around town conduct workshops on this delectable topic. Although courses may change over time, all the schools discussed in the following pages have an established history of offering chocolate-specific classes.

Quite a few of the stores mentioned earlier in this book are good sources for block chocolate and other cacao-based products that can be used in creating your own candies and desserts. For your convenience, these shops are listed at the end of this section.

Other places worth knowing about for ingredients and tools of the trade, including several lesser-known businesses recommended by top New York pastry chefs, are also described here.

Gourmand

636 South Pickett St., Alexandria, VA 22304   (800) 627-7272
Mail Order Only

THE DGF BRAND OF CHOCOLATE FROM FRANCE is chosen by many pastry chefs for its high quality and competitive price. Gourmand, a major wholesale food distributor on the East Coast, will ship orders as small as a two-kilogram bar (a little more than four pounds). The bars come in varying degrees of bitterness, from milk chocolate to unsweetened chocolate.

Gourmand also sells chocolate dessert cups, batons (the chocolate sticks that go inside a pain au chocolat), cocoa powder, and cocoa butter. Chocolate coffee beans, cigarette shavings, super-fine shavings, sprinkles, and cocoa nibs used by professionals for decorating are available, albeit in large quantities. Why not pool an order with chocolate-loving friends?

Equipment such as chocolate-dipping machines and thermometers can be ordered. Call for a catalog.

Harry Wils & Co., Inc.

182 Duane St. bet. Greenwich and Hudson Sts.   431-9731
Hours: Monday through Friday 6:00 a.m. to 2:30 p.m.; usually closed
from 12:30 p.m. to 1:00 p.m. for lunch. Call ahead; hours vary.
Prices: Inexpensive to Moderate; No Credit Cards

YOU MUST WALK UP A LOADING DOCK to enter this warehouse of specialty foods for the trade, which we discovered years ago. They have been happy to accommodate our small retail orders ever since.

Prices are rock-bottom for top-quality goods, and more important, you can buy such hard-to-find items as 10 varieties of premium Valrhona chocolate (most sold in 6.6-pound blocks) and 30 kinds of the less expensive Cacao Barry chocolate. Chocolate glazes and flakes are among the decorating items for sale. If your recipe calls for cream, buy the quart-sized containers of restaurant-quality heavy cream carried here. It whips much better than the supermarket brands.

Service is great at Harry Wils. French-born Rachel Akselrod, manager of specialty foods, is a chocolate expert, and she happily volunteers information on the subject. Call in your order at least one hour in advance. Kenny Kahn, the friendly presence behind the pick-up booth, usually answers the phone. He'll have your order waiting for you when you arrive.

Lamalle Kitchenware

36 W. 25th St. bet. Broadway and Sixth Ave., Sixth Floor   242-0730
Hours: Monday through Friday 8:30 a.m. to 5:00 p.m.
Prices: Expensive
Mail Order and Delivery Available

IT S WELL WORTH TAKING A TRIP to the Flatiron District, where on the sixth floor of an industrial building you'll find Lamalle Kitchenware, a 5,000-square-foot loft space brimming with both up-to-date and vintage kitchen tools.

Lamalle Kitchenware was established in 1927 by Charles Lamalle, who was the first to bring fine French copperware and kitchen equipment to the United States. For decades the outfit was primarily a wholesale supplier to numerous American restaurants. In 1994, Chip Fisher bought the company from the Lamalle estate, and he and co-owner Jean Tibbetts have since successfully rejuvenated the business. Both are enthusiastic and have an encyclopedic knowledge of their stock, which is the finest and most extensive of its kind in the city. Tibbetts, who has written a book on kitchen tools, is often on hand to answer questions.

Among the items you'll find at Lamalle are chocolate forks used for dipping, chocolate thermometers, garniture sets for carving, various molds, and tools for pastry making.

The New School Culinary Center

66 W. 12th St. bet. Fifth and Sixth Aves.   255-4141 (Culinary Center information); 229-5690 (registration and catalogs)

THE NEW SCHOOL holds a two-session chocolate workshop twice a year. Classes are limited to 12 students, who learn hands-on the technical aspects of working with chocolate, including how to temper chocolates and make chocolate baskets, molded candies, curls, truffles, and other treats.

In addition, a class dedicated to baking chocolate desserts is periodically scheduled.

NY Cake and Baking Center

56 W. 22nd St. bet. Fifth and Sixth Aves.   675-2253
Hours: Monday through Saturday 10:00 a.m. to 6:00 p.m.
Prices: Moderate
Mail Order Available

LOCATED IN THE HEART OF CHELSEA, this place stocks all sorts of items for the home baker, from elaborate wedding cake stands to ornaments for birthday cakes. If you are looking for something specific, they are sure to have it.

They also carry a big selection of baking chocolate, including Valrhona from France, Callebaut from Belgium, and Van

Leer—made on the other side of the Hudson River, in Jersey City. Van Leer also makes snaps, which are coin-sized pieces that can be used for decorating. They come in one-pound bags in such colors as pink, blue, red, green, yellow, and purple. Van Leer also manufactures a Dutch process cocoa powder.

Several times a year, two levels of chocolate workshops are given at the store. Students learn the art of molding, dipping, and creating various shapes in demonstration classes that include limited hands-on participation.

New York University Center for Food and Hotel Management

35 W. 4th St. bet. Greene St. and Washington Square Park
998-5588

NYU's CENTER FOR FOOD AND HOTEL MANAGEMENT offers single-session culinary workshops geared to both the enthusiast and the professional. The center periodically offers courses in chocolate that emphasize the special techniques required to work with this sometimes elusive ingredient. In one class, called "A Spring Array of Chocolate Treats," students participated in the creation of several sophisticated chocolate desserts ideal for warm weather.

Peter Kump's School of Culinary Arts

307 E. 92nd St. bet. First and Second Aves.

410-5152; (800) 522-4610

50 W. 23rd St. bet. Fifth and Sixth Aves.   242-2882

THE EVER-EXPANDING Peter Kump's School usually has something chocolate to offer, be it a special lecture or a hands-on class. Two to three times a year a chocolate dessert workshop is taught by Nick Malgieri, the author of best-selling books on baking and desserts. These classes are intensive, usually lasting about five hours and sometimes held over for several sessions.

Call the school for a free copy of *The Cooking School News* which contains complete course listings. Classes are held at the Upper East Side location and at the new facility in Chelsea.

The Sweet Life

63 Hester St. at Ludlow St.   598-0092

Hours: Sunday through Friday 10:00 a.m. to 6:00 p.m.

Prices: Inexpensive to Moderate

Mail Order Available

WE WERE SURPRISED TO DISCOVER what a big seller baking chocolate is at the Sweet Life, a plain green storefront on the

Lower East Side. The place is reminiscent of an old general store, so it looks as if it's been around since well before 1982, the year it opened.

You can buy small chunks of Merckens and various sizes of Callebaut, including the strips for pain au chocolat, half-kilo bars, and the jumbo bars used by many professionals. In fact, the store does a healthy mail order business.

The store also sells simple, inexpensive, old-fashioned dipped treats. A portable workstation is set up in a corner, and on occasion you can see the employees dipping all kinds of foods—from marshmallows and banana chips to pretzels and jelly grahams—into warmed chocolate. The items are sold loose or in convenient, individually wrapped packages. Kosher and sugar-free chocolates are also available.

Williams-Sonoma

1175 Madison Ave. at 86th St.   289-6832
Hours: Monday through Saturday 10:00 a.m. to 7:00 p.m.;
Sunday Noon to 6:00 p.m.

1309 Second Ave. at 69th St.   288-8408
Hours: Monday through Friday 10:00 a.m. to 8:00 p.m.;
Saturday 10:00 a.m. to 7:00 p.m.; Sunday Noon to 6:00 p.m.

20 E. 60th St. bet. Park and Madison Aves.   980-5155
Hours: Monday through Friday 10:00 a.m. to 7:00 p.m.;
Saturday 10:00 a.m. to 6:00 p.m.; Sunday Noon to 5:00 p.m.

110 Seventh Ave. at 17th St.   633-2203
Hours: Monday through Friday 10:00 a.m. to 8:00 p.m.;
Saturday 10:00 a.m. to 7:00 p.m.; Sunday Noon to 6:00 p.m.

580 Broadway bet. Houston and Prince Sts.   343-7330
Monday through Saturday 10:00 a.m. to 8:00 p.m.;
Sunday Noon to 7:00 p.m.
Prices: Expensive
Mail Order and Delivery Available

ALMOST EVERY MANHATTAN NEIGHBORHOOD now has a Williams-Sonoma to call its own. These upscale kitchenware stores carry everything from baking thermometers and copper pots to professional top-of-the-line French stoves.

Chocolate lovers should head straight to the packaged foods section, where they can purchase baking chocolate made by Valrhona, the most famous brand in France. It is sold in 14-ounce bars. Williams-Sonoma also carries the Belgian brand Callebaut in a giant 11-pound slab—handy for anyone who likes to bake in a big way.

Other Sources for Baking Chocolate

Index by Neighborhood

Notes

Other Titles Available From City & Company

TITLE	RETAIL
How To Find an Apartment in New York	$12.95
New York Book of Beauty (cloth)	$16.00
New York Cat Owner's Guide	$9.95
New York Book of Coffee & Cake (cloth)	$16.00
Cool Parents Guide to All of New York	$12.95
New York Book of Dance	$14.00
New York Dog Owner's Guide	$9.95
Good & Cheap Ethnic Eats	$9.95
Good & Cheap Vegetarian Dining	$9.95
Jones Guide to Fitness & Health	$9.95
Ken Druse's New York City Gardener	$15.00
How To Make New York a Better Place to Live	$9.95
How To Meet A Mensch in New York 2nd Edition	$12.00
Marden's Guide to Manhattan Booksellers	$15.00
New York Book of Music	$15.00
New York Book of Tea (cloth)	$15.00
New York's 50 Best Nightspots	$9.95
New York's 50 Best Places to Find Peace & Quiet	$9.95
New York's 50 Best Secret Architectural Treasures	$9.95
Shop NY/Downtownstyle	$15.95
Shop NY/Jewelry	$15.95
Psychic New York	$13.00
A Year In New York (cloth)	$20.00

You can find all these books at your local bookstore, or write to:
City & Company, 22 West 23rd St. New York, NY 10010
Tel: 212-366-1988

About the Authors

WILLIAM GILLEN and PATRICIA MACKENZIE became interested in chocolate while on their honeymoon in France, where they discovered the joys of good eating. For more than three years they published a monthly newsletter, *The New York Food Letter*, while spending their days on Wall Street and at Columbia Law School. Today, away from the table, Patricia MacKenzie is a consultant in the personal computer software industry, and when William Gillen is not looking for something to eat, he is employed by a major investment bank. They live on the West Side and in Columbia County, New York, and are frequent contributors to *The New York Daily News*. This is their first book.

About the Illustrator

SALLY MARA STURMAN lives, paints, and cooks in a Brooklyn brownstone that she shares with her husband, Monty, and snake, Ichi. She has illustrated the world of food for countless books and magazines. She says that *New York Chocolate Lover's Guide* has been the icing on the cake! She is represented by the Arts Counsel in New York.